THE 5-MINUTE
— MUM —
Time management for busy parents

THE 5-MINUTE
— MUM —

Time management for busy parents

Clare Shaw

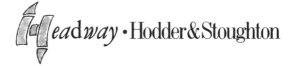

Headway · Hodder & Stoughton

Cataloguing in Publication Data is available from the British Library

ISBN 0 340 62122 2

First published 1995
Impression number   10 9 8 7 6 5 4 3 2 1
Year   1999 1998 1997 1996 1995

Typeset by Wearset, Boldon, Tyne and Wear.
Printed in Great Britain for Hodder & Stoughton Educational, a division of Hodder Headline
Plc, 338 Euston Road, London NW1 3BH by Cox & Wyman Ltd, Reading

Contents

Introduction

There is currently a steady increase in the number of women returning to work. Some are continuing in full-time employment straight after starting a family, while many others are taking up part-time work; some women are taking career breaks of varying lengths, while others are training for a whole new career after they have had a family.

Against this background we have changes in traditional family structures, with an increasing number of single parent families or families with step children. At the same time, we have families where fathers are taking an increasing role in bringing up the children. In some cases, the father is the main care taker while the mother pursues a career. The different family structures and varying working situations seem infinite, yet parents all seem to have one thing in common – they do not have enough time.

The 5-minute Mum is aimed at all parents who are trying to juggle their time between the family and other things, usually work. Perhaps it should be called *The 5-minute Mum or Dad* because it is applicable to all busy parents. The ideas outlined in the book have been used successfully by many parents to gain a feeling of control. Once we feel in control of our time, we can use it to our advantage. We need time for our family, work and ourselves and it is often this last one – ourselves – which gets left at the bottom of the heap. But it can be done. With thought and organisation and in some cases, some drastic restructuring of our lives, we can all be five-minute mums.

Throughout the book children are referred to as 'He' in some chapters and 'She' in others. The parent is usually referred to as 'She' but the information is generally applicable to mums or dads. Chapter 3 deals with child care and, for convenience, refers to most carers, particularly nannies, as female. This is the most likely scenario, although your child's carer could be male.

Finally, if you think you do not have enough time to read this book, then you clearly need to. The book does not waste your time with boring facts and figures or endless personal anecdotes. Instead, it is crammed with practical ideas and advice which you can put straight into use to the benefit of your whole family.

CHAPTER ONE

What is a Five-minute Mum?

'Never before have we had so little time in which to do so much.'

F.D. Roosevelt.

If you are a busy parent but feel in control of your time, you are a five-minute mum. If you can balance all the different aspects of your life so that everyone, including yourself, is content, then you are a five-minute mum. If you feel organised, in control and optimistic, you are a five-minute mum. And you are a five-minute mum if you can make the most of every five minutes, knowing that five minutes lounging on the couch watching a soap opera with your teenager can sometimes be as much value as five minutes organising homework, cooking the dinner and doing something creative with a toddler all at the same time. If, like many parents, you feel you are 'muddling along', that your lifestyle has taken over and that you no longer have any control of your time, then turning yourself into a five-minute mum can help you regain that control to the benefit of the whole family.

Of course, a five-minute mum may technically be a dad. The term applies to anybody who is trying to combine successful parenting with other commitments, probably work. This is often particularly difficult for a working mother for, although she may share parenting with her partner, in many cases it is her making the decisions and doing the delegating. It is therefore the working mother who needs good time management more than anyone else. Single parents, whether they are mothers or fathers, also have a difficult juggling act to perform if they are to maintain a good balance between work and parenting. And in trying to be a successful parent and get the most out of a job, there is often little time left for that parent to spend on herself or himself. The aim of good time management should not, therefore, simply be to become a better employee or a more successful parent. Being a five-minute mum means you value yourself, and part of the time-juggling act will include finding time for you.

If the five-minute mum sounds like some sort of superwoman (or superman), then nothing could be further from the truth. On the contrary, the five-minute mum knows how to cut corners, can prioritise everything in her life so that she can ignore the unimportant, and knows how to say no, so that she does not end up doing everything for everyone and nothing for herself. The five-minute mum can delegate (everything) and then go and lie in a hot, soapy bath with a large glass of wine without feeling any guilt whatsoever.

A five-minute mum accepts that things will not always go smoothly, that unexpected problems will arise and that she, herself, is far from perfect. But a five-minute mum does not aim for perfection, just a happy, balanced life where everyone feels fulfilled most of the time and nobody feels any regrets for the lifestyle that has been chosen. And if the five-minute mum still sounds too good to be true, it is worth noting that many parents have gained control of their time and therefore their life and that this option is open to anyone. All it takes is a little thought, a little planning and a lot of positive thinking. It is worth considering what exactly it is we are aiming for and what the traps are that all busy parents fall into. It will then be easier to set goals and avoid the pitfalls as we set out to achieve them.

A FIVE-MINUTE MUM AIMS TO . . .

. . . **integrate parenting with other experiences** (Chapter Seven) You may find yourself saying 'If only I had more time for the children . . .' while full-time parents with no other commitments may say 'If only I had more time for me ...'. Even a parent who does not have to work may need to for her own self-fulfilment and non-working parents need interests outside of parenting in order to maintain a balance in their lives. Recognise that you will be a better parent if you have other experiences and interests.

... involve her child in many of her own activities (Chapters Four to Six)

Try not to divide your life into different compartments. You are a parent 24 hours a day even though you will not be an active one for all of that time (hopefully). Involve your child while you are doing chores and you will be giving him your time as well as doing the necessary mundane tasks. Take your child to work with you so that he understands that you have other important commitments. By all means involve your child in your hobbies and interests but remember to have some time on your own as well.

... use her time effectively (Chapter Seven)

This does not mean that every minute is spent either working or doing something frightfully educational with your child. It means that you do not waste time taking on things you wish you had not and that you cannot cope with, that you plan your time carefully and that if you need more time to relax and do nothing, then you make room in your schedule for it.

... be aware of the advantages of short bursts of parenting (Chapters Four to Six)

Five or ten minutes playing with a toddler or chatting to a teenager can be invaluable. We can wait weeks for the opportunity to go to the beach for the day or go shopping together. Meanwhile, we have wasted all those five minutes worrying about not going out for the day instead of making the most of them.

... allow her child space and time on his own when needed (Chapter Eight)

Parents often find it easier to acknowledge that they need time to themselves than to recognise that even a very young child needs time on his own. We may have planned to spend half an hour playing with a toddler, only to find him engrossed in some experimental play of his own. We may have scheduled a chat with an older child, only to find him shut in his bedroom wanting to be by himself. Be flexible enough to change plans and do not let guilt lead you to believe that your child always needs you all the time.

... know 100 spontaneous games and activities which need no preparation (Chapters Four to Six)

Suddenly, you've got five or ten minutes before bath time. Your child wants to play with you, you want to play with your child but by the time you have decided what to do and located the necessary game, the moment has passed and it is bedtime anyway. Sometimes a cuddle, a chat or a story is ideal. At other times, something novel or spontaneous is required. Or else you may both need that familiar, personal game that only you two do together. Learning to judge the situation and read your child's mood helps you pick just the right activity.

... find parenting rewarding and relaxing (Chapter Eight)

Of course, it will not always be. But the busier you are and the more out of control of your time you are, the more likely you are to forget that parenting can be fun. When there are 50 jobs to do which should have been done yesterday, being a parent can just seem like another of those jobs. Learn to manage your time successfully so that you can enjoy the parenting as much as you deserve to.

... get rid of the guilt (Chapter Eight)

Parental guilt is often completely unfounded and can occur even when the children are happy, settled and thriving in the part-time care of someone else. We feel guilty if we are not with our children, preferably doing something stimulating and educational, all the time. Yet we know that this scenario would do neither our children nor ourselves any good. Learn to acknowledge when things are going right and remind yourself of the benefits to your child of having a busy or working mum.

... have realistic expectations of herself and her children (Chapter Eight)

No parent is perfect and perhaps it does our children good to realise this. Children do not suffer from the inevitable bout of parental tiredness, bad temper or inconsistency. Similarly, your child will not be perfect all the time so try not to blame every little bit of bad behaviour on yourself. Take an overview of the whole situation; if you and your children are generally happy and well adjusted, deal with little problems as they arise and try not to turn them into big ones.

. . . encourage her child to build good relationships with other adults (Chapters Three and Nine)

Children who are given the opportunity to relate closely to a wider circle of adults are more likely to develop good social skills and confidence. They are not as likely to be clingy and will cope with the necessary and inevitable separations from you. Ensuring that your child has some form of child care does not only benefit you, enabling you to work or carry out some of your own activities – it is also of enormous benefit to your child.

. . . maintain a good balance between work and home (Chapters Two and Seven)

There is a danger of double guilt for working parents – guilt because they feel they should spend more time with the children and guilt because they feel they should do extra hours at work. The only solution is to set priorities, work out when you are doing what and stick to it, ignoring any pleas from either side to change your priorities. Only you can set the balance between your two jobs, reviewing this balance as and when you feel it is necessary.

. . . get the most out of other people (Chapters Three and Nine)

One of the secrets of good time management is delegation. This may involve your partner, relatives and child carer. It is all too easy to half delegate, still hovering around to make sure your partner or nanny does it like you do. You may be stuck with more than your share of the decision making, but make sure the groundwork is divided up in a way that suits everyone.

. . . have a positive attitude to work and child care (Chapters Two and Three)

This involves dispensing with any unfounded guilt feelings and looking at the positive benefits to everyone. Actually write down what your child gets out of child care, what your carer gets out of it and what you get out of working. These will include short term benefits (your child is developing new self-help skills and you have extra money coming in) and long-term benefits (your child will grow up with a balanced view of women's roles and you will be progressing in your career).

... know her limitations and priorities (Chapter Seven)

You cannot continue to take on more and more responsibilities. There are only a certain number of hours in the day and you do not have unlimited energy. You will need to make priorities and learn to say no to anything else. If you want to spend more time with the children or take up a new hobby, you need to find the time by cutting out something less important.

... have a structured but flexible day (Chapter Seven)

Busy and working parents will need some structure to the day. You will have part of your time schedule set out for you – when you are due at work, and so on. However, be flexible about the other parts, particularly at weekends and on days off. Children are unpredictable and may need your attention when you are in the middle of cooking dinner, for example. If your child's needs seem to be a priority at that time, put everything else on hold. Similarly, get on with something else if he chooses not to play the game you planned but wants time on his own.

PARENT TRAPS

Having set out what our aims are, we need to be aware of the pitfalls that all busy parents fall into time and time again. Most of the time, we know we have no reason to feel guilty or blame ourselves for everything and yet we still do it. Similarly, we know perfectly well that we have set ourselves quite unreasonable goals, one of which is to be the perfect parent of a perfect child. And yet we still do it. We need to be honest with ourselves and take a more objective view of our lives. Of course, it is far easier to be objective about other people's lives and to help them reach reasonable priorities. So start by being honest and admit to the traps which most affect you. Then get together with other busy parents and talk about the difficulties and benefits of your busy lifestyles. Help to tackle the problems but tell each other when the worries, anxieties and guilt feelings are unfounded and unreasonable.

This networking might be quite informal, just a group of friends getting together for a chat. Or you might want to set up something more structured with the aim of meeting other working parents. You might do this through your job or by advertising locally. Alternatively, you may like to find out if there is a local branch of Parents at Work or Parent-Link (addresses are at the back of the book).

The Waltons syndrome

Many parents still have an image of a large family with children who are immaculately turned out and behaved; where home cooking is constantly served up on a large wooden table and eternally smiling parents have infinite hours to listen to the problems of the younger members of this perfect family. This is a myth so beware of turning it into one of your objectives.

The old bag factor

All parents and especially, it seems, working mothers will receive endless advice about parenting. This will come from friends, neighbours, relatives and anyone at the bus stop who happens to overhear that you are a working mother. Decide whose advice is of value to you and listen to it. Ignore the rest politely and then make your own decisions. Do not let the words of a well-meaning but misguided busy-body prey on your mind.

The superwoman syndrome

Do not aim to do everything perfectly. The more you want to do with your life, the more corners you will have to cut. So if you are working, have a family and want to play tennis regularly, say no to chairing the parent–teacher association. Your children will not suffer if they have supper from the chip shop once a week or if their sports kit is not ironed.

Cobweb guilt

Think back to your own childhood. What are your happiest memories? Going to the beach? Playing in the back garden with your family and friends? Or having a cobweb-free house with no dust on the skirting board? Cutting corners on housework is not a reason to feel guilty. Your children will not suffer if the kitchen cupboards are not cleaned out regularly so wait for a rainy day and all do it together as a game, even if it does not end up getting done perfectly.

Guilt shopping

Sort out any guilt feelings you have before you fall into this trap. Just because you were three minutes late collecting your child from nursery does not mean you have to go out and buy the latest train and all its accessories. And just because this is the first chance you have had to go shopping with your child for months, does not mean you have to buy every item he points at. Think of an alternative, perhaps give your child an extra cuddle, story or chat which will make you both feel better and will not cause him to hold out his hand every time you collect him.

Silly guilt

Sometimes there are justified reasons for feeling guilty. Perhaps you have been constantly late home or you have been tired and therefore snappy towards your children for over a week. In these events, a rethink about managing your time is needed. However, what about the times when you feel guilty about having time away from your children when they are clearly happy, content and settled? Perhaps you have set an unreasonable ideal (see the

Waltons Syndrome) and need to talk it over with your partner or friends.

The clingy parent

Some parents have difficulty letting go completely and find it hard to share the children with their partner or the children's carer. Remind yourself that children benefit from forming relationships with other adults and, however close those relationships may be, the parent–child relationship will always be the most special. Being a clingy parent does not help the confidence of the carer or your child. So what if someone else changes the nappy differently so long as your child is happy and well cared for?

The quality-time myth

True, the quality of the time you spend with your child is more important than the quantity. But quality time does not mean cramming as many activities as you can into the time available. There is quality to snuggling up on the couch together watching children's television and there is quality to letting your child sit and chat to you while you unwind in the bath. The quality comes from judging what you and your child need at that moment and acknowledging that you both need some time to yourselves.

The blame-it-on-the-working-mother trap

Your child may react to you going back to work or spending more time away from him. However, do not fall into the trap of blaming every mood, tantrum or problem on yourself. If your child has been going to the nursery quite happily for six months and then suddenly does not want to go one morning, it is unlikely to be a delayed reaction to your work. Try to find out what the real problem is rather than bathing yourself in undeserved guilt. If your two-year-old child suddenly starts to have tantrums, it is because he is two and not because you go out to work.

The eternal martyr

Do not be afraid to ask for help directly, especially from your partner. In an ideal world, partners, friends and relatives will all rally round to help without waiting to be asked. But they do not. So do not turn yourself into a martyr, doing everything and making sure your partner sees you doing it. Try not to drop emotional hints and hope for the best. In the end, the anger, resentment and frustration will build up inside and what could have been a polite request will turn into a row. After all, nagging is just a symptom of frustration which can sometimes be avoided. Do not be a martyr to your children either. They should help you for their own good as well as yours.

The little boxes syndrome

Life does not divide up into separate compartments or boxes so do not try to make it. You cannot try to do housework from nine to eleven o'clock and play with the children from eleven to twelve o'clock before going off to work at lunch-time. Involve your child in your other activities and involve yourself in his. Talk to your child about your job and if possible show him where you work so that he can imagine you there. Set your aims for the day but be as flexible as your routine allows about how and when these are are achieved.

The doom and gloom merchant

The most important skills required by a working or busy parent are optimism and positive thinking. If you have negative views about going out to work or leaving your child in the care of others, you will only make yourself and ultimately your child unsettled. If your negative views are founded on something that needs changing, then make positive steps to make that change. Perhaps your child care is unsatisfactory or you have problems at work. If, underneath, you know that everything is fine, talk over your negative feelings with your partner or other parents.

The office baby bore

This parent trap is not such an important one as in some ways it is really only a problem for other people. However, it is worth reminding yourself that not everyone is interested in babies and how many times they were sick in the night, or toddlers and how they are getting on with their potty training. Do have pictures of your children at work and do phone them up if this is to be part of your schedule. But beware of going on about them so much that others stop taking your work seriously. If you feel a need to chat to other working parents, set up a group to meet in the lunch hour or outside working hours.

The end-of-your-nose syndrome

Parenting is a long-term occupation and yet it is all too easy to get bogged down with short-term problems. Try to see further than the end of your nose and plan ahead, keeping as many options open as possible. What will you do for after-school care once your child leaves day nursery? What contingency plans do you have if your child or his carer are ill? At the same time keep short-term problems in perspective. Is it worth getting so bothered about one small upset at nursery, for instance, when next week it will all be forgotten?

The muddle-through policy

The busier you are, the more your time needs to be planned. Muddling through can and does work for some people but this method usually means that a lot of time is wasted or misused. It also leaves the muddle-through parent with a feeling that tasks are never-ending, that things will never get done or even that life is impossible. Muddle-through parents tend to feel out of control and are just waiting for a chance to do something for themselves. That chance will probably never come unless it is planned for. Start by making a list of things to do in the order of priority, and then gradually introduce the time-management techniques outlined in Chapter Seven.

Five-minute checklist:
Are you a five-minute mum?

◆ Do you find it difficult to relax and play with your child when there is ironing or cleaning waiting to be done?

◆ Do you manage to get everything done without the aid of a list?

◆ Do you check your partner when he is with the children to make sure that he is 'doing it properly'?

◆ Have you ever agreed to do something and then regretted saying yes?

◆ Have you ever bought your child sweets or toys to 'make it up to him'?

◆ Are meal times rushed?

◆ Do you iron the sheets, underwear or night wear?

◆ Do you ever feel disappointed when your child says goodbye happily and does not rush straight over to greet you when you collect him?

◆ Do you wish you could be with your children all the time?

◆ Do you want the children out from under your feet while you get the meal ready?

◆ Do you take part in any interests, hobbies or social activities away from work and family?

◆ You are taking your child to school/nursery/the child minder. Do you feel relaxed enough to chat, play games or sing together?

◆ Does your pre-school child have a favourite job he likes to help with and does your school child have some of his own chores?

◆ You have planned a picnic but it is raining. Can you

IMMEDIATELY THINK OF AN ALTERNATIVE BUT EQUALLY EXCITING
PLAN?

◆ DOES YOUR CHILD KNOW WHERE YOU WORK AND WHAT YOU DO
THERE?

◆ DO YOU HAVE A SPECIAL TIME WITH YOUR CHILD EACH DAY, PERHAPS
AT BEDTIME, WHEN YOU CAN RELAX, CHAT OR READ A STORY?

◆ CAN YOU TOTALLY IGNORE UNWANTED ADVICE?

◆ DO YOU HAVE A CONTINGENCY PLAN FOR WHEN CARERS LET YOU
DOWN?

◆ DO YOU HAVE A CONTINGENCY PLAN FOR WHEN YOUR CHILD IS ILL?

◆ DO YOU PLAN AHEAD?

A five-minute mum would probably answer 'no' to the first ten
questions and 'yes' to the rest. However, if you did this, do make
sure that you are being completely honest with yourself.
Remember that a five-minute mum does not aim for perfection
and is aware of her own limitations and downfalls. Few people will
give ten no answers and ten yes answers; the important thing is to
be aware of where you need more organisation, balance and realistic expectations. All parents will feel unnecessarily guilty on occasions, but it is important that this does not get totally
unreasonable or totally out of control. Similarly, we all wish we
had more time with our children from time to time, but if we are
honest and realistic, we will not be aiming to be 24-hour mums.

CHAPTER TWO

Work Options

'I go to work to escape the pressures of family life and come home again to escape the pressures of work.'

Sara Welch

While you are pregnant, or even before, you will need to make decisions and arrangements concerning your return to work. This is entirely personal and will depend upon your financial needs as well as your career preferences. Regardless of whether you decide to take a career break or return as soon as possible, or whether you intend to work full or part time, early organisation is the key. Good time management means sorting out both your work and child care options well in advance, although if it is your first baby you will need to keep your options open – you will not know exactly how you are going to feel until after the event. Whatever your circumstances, avoid last minute panics to find child care and remember to let your employer know about your changed circumstances and preferences for future employment.

MATERNITY LEAVE

If you become pregnant then you are entitled to keep your job after you have the baby unless your employer employs less than five people.

Every woman who is in work when she is pregnant is entitled to 14 weeks' maternity leave. If you have worked for the same employer for two years full time, or five years part time (8 to 16 hours a week), you are entitled to 40 weeks' maternity leave.

The earliest you can start the leave is eleven weeks before the baby is due but you can work longer if you wish. However, if you have a pregnancy-related illness in the last six weeks you may have to start your maternity leave then.

You need to write to your employer at least 21 days before your maternity leave informing them of when your baby is due and telling them that you intend to return to work. Enclose a copy of your maternity certificate (form MAT B1 from your GP/midwife) if requested.

If you are taking the 40 weeks' maternity leave, let your employer know the date of your return to work at least 21 days in advance.

If you are dismissed because of being pregnant, you can claim unfair dismissal or claim that you are a victim of sexual discrimination. Contact the Equal Opportunities Commission for advice (address at back of book) or ask your local Citizen's Advice Bureau for help.

All pregnant women have the right to paid time off work to attend antenatal appointments including antenatal classes. If you have problems with this you can make a complaint to an industrial tribunal (form and information can be obtained from your unemployment office).

You can change your mind – it is quite in order to say you will return to work but change your mind later. This may involve returning maternity payments.

Get further details from The Maternity Alliance or The Equal Opportunity Commission (addresses at back of book).

MATERNITY PAY AND BENEFITS

If by 15 weeks before the week your baby is due you have worked for the same employer for at least 26 weeks you are normally entitled to Statutory Maternity Pay. This is paid for up to 18 weeks. Your entitlement will partly depend on how much you earn.

Write to your employers at least three weeks before you stop work asking for the Statutory Maternity Pay.

If you are not entitled to the Statutory Maternity Pay, you may be entitled to a Maternity Allowance. Get form MA1 from your antenatal clinic or social security office.

You are entitled to free dental treatment and prescriptions while you are pregnant and until your baby is one year old.

You may be entitled to other benefits if you are low paid or a single parent. Ask at your local benefit agency.

You will be entitled to child benefit – an application form can be obtained from the social security office.

Further details are available from The Maternity Alliance, The Department of Social Security or Department of Health Publications Unit (addresses at back of book).

THE FIVE-MINUTE PREGNANCY

Convert a calender into a chart with key dates marked. You will then know when to write to your employer, when to claim your various rights and when your maternity leave is likely to be.

Allow yourself more time to do things while you are pregnant – your health comes first.

Many pregnant women complain of forgetting things or becoming vague. Write everything down and keep it all together so that nothing gets lost or forgotten.

Do not leave everything until the last minute. You may not feel like shopping for nappies or decorating the nursery three days before the baby is due.

Make a list of everything that needs to be bought or done before the baby arrives. Put it in order of priority and highlight anything that you can delegate to a friend or partner.

If you are going to hospital to have your baby, have arrangements for other children worked out well in advance and keep key numbers by the telephone. Pack your hospital bag at least three weeks before your baby is due.

Have everything for the baby ready at home for when you come out of hospital. Make sure your partner is also prepared and has organised the necessary time off work.

Accept all offers of help.

WORK CHOICES

You will have thought about this while you are pregnant and probably even before. You may be lucky enough to have several options open to you but your decision about whether and how much to work when you have a family will probably be based on the following.

♦ **Finances**: You may have to work full time to support your family.
♦ **Personal choice**: You may enjoy work and have no desire to give it up or change your hours. Be open-minded if you are expecting your first child.
♦ **Your employer**: It may be possible to cut your hours, work flexitime or job share.
♦ **Your career**: You may feel a career break will hold you back or leave you out of date should you want to return later. Talk to your employer about re-training schemes, should you decide to take a fairly long career break.
♦ **Your partner**: Your partner may be in a better position to change hours or work flexitime. You will need to discuss all the options together as you will need to support each other if you both work.
♦ **Child care**: You will only be able to return to work happily if you feel confident about your child care arrangements. You need to take the cost of child care into account when you do your sums.

Full time

You may choose to return to full-time employment. In this case, you will need good child care arrangements and a support network of friends and family. Your child care needs to be considered well in advance, even before you have your baby. If working full time means extra money above what you need to live on, you can use the money to delegate cleaning and gardening which will buy you more time with your child.

Part time

It may be possible to do the same job but for fewer hours. Discuss part-time prospects with your employer well in advance. You may have to change job in order to do the hours you want and will, in any event, be taking a cut in salary. This is ideal for those who cannot bear to give up work totally but who want to spend more hours with their child. Set hours are usually easiest for making child care arrangements work. You may want to think ahead to the nursery and school years and do the sort of hours which will fit in with your child's education.

Flexitime

This may enable you to return to the same job but working the hours which suit you and your partner. It is difficult to get a child minder or nursery to have a flexitime arrangement but it may enable your partner to take more part in child care. He could, for instance, drop the children off at nursery while you start work early, enabling you to finish earlier and spend some time with the children later in the day.

Term-time working

This clearly lends itself to jobs in education but is now a much wider possibility. Clearly, once your children are at school then working school hours eliminates the need for any further child care arrangements.

Job sharing

This may enable you to return to the same job or to do a job at a similar level but to share the post with someone else. Your employer may already know someone you could job share with, you may meet someone expecting a baby at the same time as you or you may advertise for a job share partner. Job share hours can be flexible, or can mean working half the week or half days or alternate weeks.

Night shifts or evening work

This may enable you to work while your partner is at home to look after the children. However, it will mean spending less time with your partner. You both need to be aware of the pros and cons of this arrangement.

Working from home

This will often mean that your hours are also flexible. However, do not expect to work and look after a baby or toddler at the same time. It will probably mean using some sort of child care but as this could be in your own home with you present, you may feel happier about this type of arrangement. Working from home may mean being self-employed. It can also mean teleworking, in other words, working from home but linked to your company by telephone and fax. A telecottage allows you to work from home but share some of the equipment at a central base in your area. This has the added advantage of keeping you in touch with other workers, possibly working parents. Contact ACRE (Action with Communities in Rural England) or The Women Returners' Network for further information (addresses at back of book).

Retraining

It may be that your job does not lend itself to the type of hours you would like to work. You might consider doing a different job which could involve some sort of retraining. You can take advice from your local job centre or training colleges. It may be possible to get a grant to retrain or to update your existing training if you have had a career break.

Grants may be available from your local education authority or you may be etitled to a state bursary from the Department of

Education and Science, which publishes a useful guide. The Manpower Service Commission (number in the telephone book) gives some grants for its own job training schemes. Contact the National Institute of Adult Continuing Education for advice (address at back of book).

Career break

You may decide to take a break from work for the first year or so of your child's life. Find out from your employers or job centre if there is any training you can do either when you return or during your break.

If you are having difficulty persuading your employer to try either flexitime or job sharing, contact New Ways To Work or Parents at Work. Other useful sources of information, particularly with regards to training are Women Returners' Network and The Department of Employment who can also advise on career development loans (addresses at back of book).

Looking for work

You may not have a particular job you wish to return to and so are starting from scratch. Careers advice is available from your local careers office, job centre or in books and pamphlets in the library. You can also get advice from the Manpower Services Commission Employment Division, and can find a local number in your telephone directory. Local jobs will be advertised in the job centre, local newspapers and trade journals. You may even consider writing to any local organisations expressing an interest in working for them. In the meantime, you might consider doing some voluntary work as a step back to employment. Your local library will have a directory of voluntary organisations, both local and national. Your job centre should also be able to help you.

If you are keen to start your own business, the Women's Enterprise Development Agency may be a good source of help (address at back of book).

WORK PROBLEMS

There are potential problems during the period of adjustment when you return to work. However, always remind yourself of the good things about working to maintain a balanced view of your lifestyle. Money will be an obvious incentive but you will also have a degree of independence and self-worth. There may be social advantages to going out to work and mixing with friends and colleagues. You may be maintaining and progressing within a career and you will certainly be living your life to the full. There are also advantages to your child as she learns to relate to other adults and socialise with other children, developing good skills of independence. Even your partner will gain not only from your financial input and from the fact that you feel fulfilled but also in skills of parenting as he necessarily has to 'do his bit' with the family. When both parents work, family life will not always run completely smoothly but always look at the problems with the positive aspects of work in mind.

Problems for you

Tiredness

This is most likely if you return to work when your baby is still very young. You will have had a tremendous emotional upheaval followed by broken nights and the natural anxiety which comes in the early months. Cut down on as much as you can during the first few weeks back at work. Eat convenience foods and have realistic expectations about what you can do around the house. Delegate as much as you can and make sure your partner shares the night waking if this is still a factor. Do not give up too soon: part of the tiredness is caused by the anxieties associated with returning to work after a break. This should lessen once you get settled into a routine.

Stresses at work

Make sure you leave these at work. You now have to change into a parent on your way home and leave all the work problems behind you. Try to make friends with other working parents who will understand how you feel.

Separation from your child

This can occur whether or not your child has difficulty separating from you. It is bound to take time to adjust to leaving your child with someone else, particularly after a long career break. Try not to cling on to your child when you say goodbye – she will react to your anxieties. As you learn to trust your child's carers, you will find it easier. Always try to focus on what your child gains from being in the care of others for part of the time. You may also need to remind yourself that as a parent you are special to your child even if he seems to spend more time with the child minder!

Guilt

This is almost inevitable at some time but is rarely justified. Chapter 8 deals with this in detail.

Time management

Good time-management skills will reduce anxiety for you and your child. It should help with the stresses, tiredness and practical problems of returning to work. Chapter 7 deals with this in detail.

Practicalities

There may be practical problems to do with getting to work on time, finding suitable child care and coping when your child is ill. You will need to be prepared for any eventuality. Try to build up a support network of friends and family to help with any last minute crises. Have everything planned before your first day back at work, even down to doing a 'dummy run' of your new routine.

Retrophobia

A fear of returning to work. This largely refers to the lack of confidence many parents feel after a career break. If there are any courses available appropriate to your work, this can be a good step back. Even an assertiveness course can help. Remember, too, that being a parent will have given you qualities which will transfer to the work place. These qualities include efficiency, the ability to do more than one thing at a time, responsibility, maturity, sensitivity and enthusiasm.

Problems for your child

Separation

How your child reacts will largely depend on her age. There are likely to be one or two hiccups as she adjusts but do give it time before calling it a problem. Chapter 3 looks at this in greater detail.

Tiredness

Your child may feel more tired as she adjusts to a new routine. Again, do give it time. It is worth getting your child into her new routine before you start work so he does not suddenly have to get up much earlier or cope with a shorter nap during the day.

Less time with you

This is more likely to be a problem for you than your child. The time she does spend with you will be quality time – you will both want to make the most of it. She will also be gaining from learning to relate to other adults and children.

Difficulty relating to carer

Choose your child minder or nursery carefully and make sure the carers and your child know each other before the new routine starts. Chapter 3 looks at how to choose appropriate child care.

Imagined problems

If your child is happy and adjusts well to the new situation, do not look for problems. Most children have very few and it is this unjustified parental guilt which leads us to imagine problems where there are none.

THE NATIVITY PLAY DILEMMA

There are bound to be times when you need to be at your child's school or nursery and at work simultaneously. You know this is going to occur so be prepared for it well in advance. You will need to consider the following:

◆ Remember that school events are few and far between, probably a sport's day in the summer and a nativity play or equivalent in the winter. Make sure your boss is aware of the rarity of these events.

◆ Ask your school to let you know of such events well in advance so that you can plan ahead.

◆ Does it matter whether both parents go or would your child be happy with one who could perhaps arrange to video the event on behalf of the other?

◆ Decide whether it is most appropriate to take a half-day's leave or whether you can make up the hours later.

◆ Beware of double guilt – guilt if you are not at the school event and guilt if you miss an important meeting at work. Decide on your priority for each occasion and stick to it.

YOUR PARTNER'S OPTIONS

Should you decide to return to work after having a baby, your partner's lifestyle will necessarily change as well. You will need to discuss this in advance so that you both agree on your changing roles. Your partner may also have options about cutting down on work hours or job sharing. He may want to discuss the possibility of paternity leave with his employer or taking time off when a child is ill. There seems to be an unwritten law that it is the mothers who should take time off for doctor's appointments or sport's day. There also seems to be an unwritten law in some professions that men who are good at their job work longer than the specified number of hours. It may be that with good time management both working parents can do a good job *and* get away on time. Both you and your partner may like to get the support of other working parents of both sexes in your place of work so that a better tolerance and understanding is created amongst employers and the workforce.

DEALING WITH YOUR EMPLOYER

Do not be unrealistic about what to expect from your employer. You will not get a sympathetic attitude to sick children if you spend all morning on the phone to your daughter and the rest of the day passing round photographs of her.

Beware of turning into a baby bore. Your employers will not feel you are committed to your job if you can only talk about nappies and sleepless nights.

Be honest whenever possible. Beware of the trap of going off sick to see little Jenny's concert only to sit next to the boss's wife.

Make sure that you have a back-up system should your child care arrangements break down. Know exactly what you would do in the event of the nanny or child minder being ill.

Discuss the idea of setting up a working parents group with your employer. Or you might want to do it outside work to include other parents in your area. This can create a useful and supportive network. Check if there is already a local branch of Parents at Work (national address at back of book).

Discuss flexitime or job sharing with your employer. Just because it has not been done before, does not mean it cannot be done now.

Make sure you get to work on time. You need to allow for the possibility of your baby being sick on your shoulder just as you are about to leave and your toddler needing to show you how the tadpoles have grown when you drop her off at nursery.

Take note of the ideas for managing your time in Chapter 7. Show your employer that you can be efficient without working extra hours.

Be assertive. Learn how to say no to extra hours if you do not want them. Make it clear if your days off are inflexible.

You may want to look into the possibility of a work place nursery being set up. Chapter 3 discusses ways of going about this.

Your child is bound to be sick from time to time. Be prepared to use some holiday time to look after her. Discuss the possibility of unpaid leave to cope with emergencies such as a sick child or carer. Beware of taking work home, although this could be used to make up time on sports day and the like.

WHAT DOES YOUR CHILD GAIN FROM THE FACT THAT YOU WORK?

Parents answered . . .

'A more patient and tolerant mother.'
> Jenny Heath, chartered accountant.

'We would have to miss out on holidays without my salary.'
> Heather Smith, pharmacist.

'I feel the children are better at organising themselves.'
> Winnie Taylor, speech and language therapist.

'The experience of playing with children of his own age.'
> Andrea Logan, administrative assistant.

'Confidence and independence.'
> Shona Battensby, projects assistant.

'Because I am happy to be working now, I feel Euan is happier.'
> Karen Dodds, chiropodist.

'My children are now more self sufficient and emotionally strong.'
> Janet Tibble, nursery manager.

'My sons have gained a better respect for women. Colin is proud to have a mum doing an important job.'
> Kathy Sherrit, therapist.

'A more contented mum and the little extras in life.'
> Fiona Rust, physiotherapist.

'Having to take a share in household jobs.'
> Anne Bird, health visitor.

'Family weekends, as we have all had our own time during the week.'
> Anon., computer analyst.

'Duncan is more independent and resourceful'
> Diana Smith, shop assistant.

'A mum who is not bored, frustrated and counting the pennies.'
> Lynne Macleod, offices and building services supervisor.

'Fergus' development is further advanced than most children of his age and I am sure this has to do with his nursery experience. I also have experts (at the nursery) to ask for advice.'
> Valerie Cooper, physiotherapist

TIME TIPS

- ◆ Jobs at home will have expanded to fit the time available. You may be concerned that you will not find the time to work. Do not worry – just list the non-essential things you do and what can be delegated, which includes some of the child care.
- ◆ Invest time in making the right decision – it will save you from wasting your time doing the wrong thing. Write the pros and cons down on a large piece of paper, put them in order of priority and give a mark out of ten according to how important each consideration is.
- ◆ Do a trial run to work, via the child minder or nursery if necessary, but make sure it is at the time you will normally be travelling. Time it and add five or ten minutes for unforeseen circumstances. This is your travel time.
- ◆ Use your lunch hour wisely when you return to work. Time spent relaxing will make you more efficient in the afternoon and a more ready parent at the end of the day.

- Get into the list-making habit while you are pregnant. It will help you through the forgetful months of pregnancy and will become an essential habit if you become a working parent.
- Working flexitime or sharing care arrangements with your partner will require a large desk diary or calender.
- Make a list of your priorities while you are at home and then write down how these will need to change when you return to work. This will prepare you for re-allocating your time.
- Start using the nappy delivery service before you return to work. Can anything else be delivered?
- Working from home requires a high level of self-discipline. Stick to your pre-arranged working hours whether or not there is a pile of dirty cups in the sink and a TV covered in dust.
- The after-work drink may become a thing of the past or at least it will have to be scheduled in. Arrange with your partner times when you can both socialise with your respective colleagues.

FIVE-MINUTE CHECKLIST: WHEN TO GO BACK TO WORK

Deciding if and when to return to work may be a difficult decision for some mothers. For others, there will simply be no choice or they may just know exactly what they want. Ask yourself these questions to help you make a considered decision.

- COULD YOU MANAGE FINANCIALLY WITHOUT YOUR WAGE OR WITH A CUT IN WAGES?

- ARE YOU HAPPY TO GIVE UP THOSE LITTLE EXTRAS TOWARDS WHICH YOUR MONEY CONTRIBUTED?

◆ HAVE YOU TAKEN INTO ACCOUNT THE COST OF CHILD CARE AND TRAVEL TO WORK WHEN DOING YOUR SUMS?

◆ WOULD YOU HAVE MONEY TO SPARE TO SPEND ON A CLEANER OR GARDENER?

◆ ARE YOU CONFIDENT YOU WILL FIND GOOD CHILD CARE?

◆ WOULD YOU SPEND ALL YOUR WORKING HOURS WORRYING ABOUT THE WELFARE OF YOUR CHILD?

◆ CAN YOU VISUALISE YOURSELF IN THE COMPANY OF OTHER PARENTS AT THE MOTHER AND TODDLER GROUP?

◆ IS IT REALISTIC TO EXPECT TO CONTINUE SOCIALISING WITH OLD WORK COLLEAGUES? WHAT HAPPENED TO OTHER NEW PARENTS WHO LEFT?

◆ WOULD FULL-TIME PARENTING LEAVE YOU HAPPY AND FULFILLED?

◆ HAVE YOU ALWAYS LOOKED FORWARD TO RETURNING TO WORK AFTER A HOLIDAY?

◆ COULD YOU COMPENSATE FOR THE LACK OF ADULT COMPANY AND STIMULATION BY ATTENDING AN EVENING CLASS OR CLUB?

◆ IS YOUR PARTNER IN FULL AGREEMENT WITH THE HOURS YOU WISH TO WORK OR WILL THIS BE AN AREA OF CONFLICT?

◆ IS YOUR PARTNER AWARE OF THE CONTRIBUTION TO PARENTING HE WILL HAVE TO MAKE? DOES HE FEEL POSITIVE ABOUT THIS?

◆ DO YOU AGREE THAT CHILDREN HAVE MUCH TO GAIN FROM BUILDING RELATIONSHIPS WITH OTHER ADULTS AND CHILDREN?

◆ WOULD YOU BE HAPPY TO TAKE A CAREER BREAK IF IT WAS ONLY FOR A FINITE AMOUNT OF TIME?

◆ DO YOU FEEL STRONGLY THAT BABIES NEED A SPECIFIC AMOUNT OF TIME AT HOME WITH A PARENT BEFORE ADAPTING TO HAVING TWO WORKING PARENTS?

◆ DO YOU HAVE CLOSE FRIENDS AND RELATIVES TO PROVIDE A SUPPORT NETWORK?

◆ DO YOU HAVE A STRONG GUT FEELING ABOUT WHAT YOU REALLY WANT?

◆ Does it worry you that your child might take her first steps or say her first words when you are not there?

◆ Given the choice, would you rather not work at all?

◆ Do you have a rosy view of family life with perfect children of a perfect mother who bakes bread and makes gingham dresses?

◆ Did your own mother go out to work? Has this influenced your view of what family life should be?

◆ Do you have an open mind so that if it does not work out, you have a contingency plan?

Answering these questions should help you to focus on what you really want. It also helps to write down all your thoughts on the matter as they come into your head. Then sort them out into pros and cons. The thoughts that came to you first are likely to be the most important to you.

CHAPTER THREE

Child Care Choices

'They were glad Katie Nanna had gone, for they had never liked her. She was old and fat and smelt of Barley Water ... "Mary Poppins is the only person I want in the world!" wailed Michael.'

(From Mary Poppins by P.L. Travers)

When you return to work it is essential to find good and appropriate care for your child. If your child is happy and settled, so will you be. It is worth planning ahead – good child minders and nurseries are more likely to be booked up early than indifferent ones. You may also need time to find out what is available especially if you are new to the area or it is your first child. Take time to look at all the options, get opinions from other parents and plan ahead so that the child care you choose will still be suitable in six months' time. You may also want to think ahead to when your child's needs are likely to change.

CHILD MINDERS

A child minder looks after children in her own home and the hours and fees are negotiable. A child minder must, by law, be registered with the local social services department. They will inspect her home to make sure it is safe and lay down a limit to the number of children she can mind at any one time. This is often restricted to three children under five (including her own) with only one baby under age one allowed. She may provide after-school care for older children. A typical minder has her own children and minds others to supplement her income. She tends to see her role as caring for the child's physical needs rather than providing any educational activities.

Advantages and disadvantages

- ◆ The hours are likely to be flexible.
- ◆ The cost is usually reasonable.
- ◆ Your child only has to build up a relationship with one new adult and a few other children.
- ◆ The minder may be prepared to take your child to and from playgroup or appointments.
- ◆ The arrangements are likely to cover school holidays.
- ◆ Your child has the opportunity to stay on even after starting school with just an adjustment to the hours.
- ◆ The minder is unlikely to take your child if he is unwell.
- ◆ Most child minders provide good physical care but not necessarily educational stimulation.
- ◆ Most child minders are not qualified.
- ◆ If your child minder is ill, you may be left without care for a time.

How to choose

- ◆ A list of child minders is available from the local social services department. Pick several to visit which are near your home or work. Alternatively you could look for adverts in the local shops or press. Or you could get recommendations from friends or anyone you can corner at the clinic or parent and baby group.
- ◆ Visit at least three child minders checking first that places are likely to be available for the hours you require.
- ◆ Before you visit, enquire whether the minder is registered with social services. Do not bother to visit if she is not. Ask to see her certificate of registration, which will indicate how many children she can mind. Also check that she has a public liability insurance policy.
- ◆ At the visit, note if the children seem happy and settled. Take

a note of the general atmosphere. Always try to visit when the other children are likely to be there.

♦ Check that she has safety equipment such as a stair gate, cooker guard, plug guards and fire extinguisher. Social services should have looked into all safety aspects. Ask if the child minder has any first-aid experience.

♦ Discuss the daily routine. What happens at meal times? Do the children play outside or have any outings? If there are to be outings, ask about travelling arrangements. Are there plenty of safe and appropriate toys?

♦ Ask about anything you feel strongly about, such as whether there are pets or anyone in the house who smokes.

♦ Take your child with you and note how the minder relates to him.

♦ Ask if the minder is prepared to take your child to any medical or clinic appointments, if this is important to you.

♦ What about naps during the day – are there facilities for this?

♦ Ask if she is prepared to keep supplies of your nappies and spare clothes there. Taking your baby to the child minder's can end up feeling like moving house every morning.

♦ Some child minders offer to provide meals or snacks for the children. Would you prefer to provide your own?

♦ Ask if there is an emergency arrangement with another child minder in case she is ill.

♦ Be clear about the cost and holiday arrangements right from the start.

♦ Take notes during or immediately after your visit so that you can compare the different minders.

♦ Visit again when the child minder is not expecting you.

Making it work

♦ When you have chosen your child minder, draw up a written contract which will include details of hours, fees, charges for absences and holidays, medical details and any particular requirements you have. The National Childminding Association (address at back of book) has contracts available.

Be prepared to pay a retainer to keep your place available.

◆ Make sure you always keep your side of the bargain by collecting your child on time and paying promptly.

◆ Most child minders will respect your requests, such as no sweets or limited television, but do not be too demanding. She is looking after other children too and may already have an established routine.

◆ Do not send your child in when he is very ill. That is unfair to the child as well as the child minder and any other children in her home.

◆ If possible, arrange for your child to have his first session there before you return to work so that you can spend time settling him in and so that the first session can be a little shorter.

◆ Contact the National Childminding Association for further information (address at back of book).

Nurseries

Sending your child to a nursery means that he will be in a larger group of children cared for by qualified personnel. A day nursery is normally open long hours and takes all pre-school children, including young babies. A place in a state-run day nursery is hard to come by although priority is given to families with particular social or medical problems. They are run by social services and are staffed by nursery nurses. Private day nurseries also have to be registered with social services and, again, places may be hard to come by. Private nursery schools may be less flexible in their hours but could be open at least for school hours. They may only take children from three years. You would need to get details from each nursery school. The staff will include nursery teachers as well as assistants. State-run nursery schools/classes normally offer your child three or more half day sessions a week. This may suit if you are working part time or if you have a child minder willing to collect your child. You may be lucky enough to have a work place nursery or your employer may have an arrangement with a local nursery.

Advantages and disadvantages

◆ You are not relying on one person who may be ill one day.
◆ Nurseries normally provide a very safe environment for your child.
◆ The staff are qualified in caring for children and are likely to offer some educational stimulation.
◆ They do not always shut for holiday time.
◆ The ratio of children to staff may be more than at a child minder's.
◆ You would not expect a nursery to take your child to medical or dental appointments.
◆ Private nurseries may be expensive although prices vary.
◆ The hours may be less flexible than at a child minder.

How to choose

◆ The local social services department will have details of day nurseries. Your health visitor may also be able to help.
◆ The education authority will have details of nursery schools. The library may also keep a register.
◆ Look on notice boards in the library, health centre and Post Office.
◆ Consult Yellow Pages or contact the British Association for Early Childhood Education (address at back of book).
◆ Visit nurseries in convenient locations which suit the hours you need.
◆ If you are choosing a nursery school, you may want to think ahead to which school your child will attend so that he will move up with some of the same children.
◆ Ask what qualifications the staff have and about the staff–child ratio.
◆ Look at the equipment and accommodation. Is there enough room for messy play or playing outside?
◆ Ask what the nursery aims to do. Will the day be structured and include some learning activities?
◆ At the visit, note your child's reaction and the reaction of the adults to him.

◆ Take note of your gut feeling and intuition.
◆ Try to talk to other parents who send their children there.

Making it work

◆ Arrange in advance whether you are going to stay to settle your child in on the first occasion.
◆ Pay on time and be on time to collect your child.
◆ If you have any major concerns, ask for an appointment to see the head of the nursery. Do not expect her to talk for half an hour at the end of each day.
◆ Make sure that the nursery has your daytime telephone number and your child's medical details.

PLAYGROUPS

Most playgroups do not claim to be a form of child care and normal playgroup hours do not suit. However, there are now some playgroups which do stay open for longer hours. The Pre-school Playgroups Association (address at back of book) can advise if there are any such groups in your area. Most playgroups rely on help from parents, which is arranged on a rota basis. If you are unable to help, point this out when you visit and offer to help in other ways, such as with fund raising. The same criteria for selection apply as for choosing a nursery.

NANNIES

A nanny is trained in child care and will look after your child in your own home. She will be responsible for everything to do with the child including preparing his meals and keeping his room clean. She would not normally do other household duties. You may want a nanny to live in or out, or it may be appropriate to share her with another family.

Advantages and disadvantages

◆ Your child stays in his own environment so is likely to feel secure.

◆ Your child has the opportunity of building up a close relationship with one adult.

◆ A nanny should be prepared to take your child to playgroup or nursery so that contact with other children is maintained.

◆ You have more say over what your child does each day and can intervene if you feel strongly about something, such as his diet or behaviour.

◆ A good nanny may be expensive, although if you share one or have a large family yourself, it may compare well to other forms of child care.

◆ Even nannies get ill so you will need a contingency plan.

◆ You are an employer and must take on all the necessary responsibility and paper work.

How to choose

◆ You can use an agency which will do all the work for you, including drawing up the contract. This will involve a one-off payment.

◆ You can advertise nationally (The Lady magazine is most suitable, or Nursery World) or locally, specifying exactly what you are looking for. Put yourself in the nanny's position when writing the advert – what does she need to know?

◆ You will probably want a nanny who is NNEB trained (National Nursery Examination Certificate – a two year course). Other recognised qualifications are the BTEC (Business and Technical Education Council) diploma in nursery nursing, NAMCW City and Guilds (National Association of Maternal and Child Welfare), RSA for nursery nurses or SVQ (Scottish Vocational Qualification) in childcare and education. You can contact the Norland, Chiltern or Princess Christian private nursery training colleges (addresses at back of book). Nannies from these colleges are highly trained and therefore more expensive.

◆ Speak to applicants on the telephone first to eliminate any who do not meet your essential criteria.

◆ Interview the prospective candidates in person and draw up a short list. Then re-interview. If the nanny turns up on her first day with a large dog and a cigarette hanging out of her mouth, you have not interviewed her properly.

◆ Take up references which must include the immediate previous employer. Try to speak to referees on the telephone if possible.

◆ Take proper notes at the interview – not just scribbled crayon on the back of an envelope. These are essential when you are going to interview several candidates.

◆ Note how each applicant responds to your child.

◆ Ask about previous jobs and views on child-rearing as well as anything that is particularly important to you.

◆ Let her ask you any questions.

◆ Be totally clear about the hours to be worked, time off, payment and duties.

Making it work

◆ Take a nanny on for a trial period of one or two months.

◆ Discuss strong views on areas such as diet, discipline or potty training right at the beginning, rather than trying to change things later.

◆ Be friendly but not so much so that giving instructions becomes difficult.

◆ Stick to the terms of employment, be friendly and deal with grievances straight away. Try not to knock her confidence. Give praise where it's due.

◆ Do not treat her as a general dogsbody. Do not be consistently late home. Do not encroach on her time off.

◆ You will be responsible for your nanny's tax, National Insurance and sick pay. The Inland Revenue will provide all the details of how to deal with this. You will need the simplified domestic PAYE scheme card and details of National Insurance contributions.

◆ Do your sums carefully. Sometimes you can pay your nanny less and yet her take home pay is more. She will not be liable for tax if she earns less than the lower earnings limit for National Insurance contributions. Your local social security office can give you up-to-date figures.

◆ You will need to send her P45 and address of last employer to the tax office. If this is her first post, she will need to fill in form P46, also available from the Inland Revenue.

◆ A nanny can be self-employed and sort out her own tax contributions.

◆ You will also need a written contract by law. A suggested contract is available from The Federation of Recruitment and Employment Services (address at back of book). This will include details of hours, duties, holidays and giving notice to leave.

◆ You will need to notify your household and motor insurers. If the nanny is a member of the Professional Association of Nursery Nurses, she is automatically insured against your child having an accident due to her negligence.

◆ If you are sharing a nanny, you must register with the social services because she is then classified as a child minder.

◆ You could ask the nanny to keep a simple daily diary so you know what to talk to your child about at the end of the day. This can enable you to keep control of the daily routine.

◆ Sack the nanny if necessary.

Mother's helps

Mother's helps are basically unqualified nannies who will do a combination of housework and child care in your own home. This is probably a suitable arrangement for older children who may be at nursery or school some of the time.

Advantages and disadvantages

◆ Mother's helps are generally cheaper than a qualified nanny.
◆ They are usually willing to do other household chores.

- Their hours will be flexible.
- The child remains in his own home.
- A mother's help's experience will vary – it may be limited to bringing up her own children.
- They will still need a contract of employment and, depending on the hours and pay, you may be responsible for tax and National Insurance.

How to choose

- Advertise in local papers or shops.
- Interview in the same way as you would for a nanny.
- Do not expect too much from an unqualified mother's help – on the other hand you may be lucky enough to find a 'gem'.
- Have a written contract outlining hours and duties.

Making it work

- Make sure your help has all the appropriate daytime contact numbers.
- Be friendly and fair.
- Do not expect your help to clean the whole house and look after a young child at the same time. Be realistic in your expectations.

AU PAIRS

An au pair is unmarried and aged between 17 and 27, according to immigration rules. The immigration office lists appropriate countries which includes all those in the EEC. A non-EEC au pair will require a work permit. Home Office guide-lines indicate that the au pair works for up to five hours a day in return for pocket money. The work can include domestic duties and child care but she should be allowed time off to attend language classes. Further information is available from the Home Office, Immigration and Nationality Department (address at back of book).

Advantages and disadvantages

◆ There is not as much administration as for a nanny – no
   contract is needed as in effect she only gets pocket money and
   board and lodging. She will not earn enough to involve tax
   payments.

◆ Low wages – as the au pair will only work up to five hours a
   day, paying a low 'pocket money' wage is quite acceptable.

◆ The au pair must live in and should be prepared to babysit
   twice a week.

◆ Your child may get the opportunity to learn about other
   cultures and languages.

◆ Normally the au pair's stay is limited to two years although
   this can be extended, especially for EEC nationals.

◆ You may not have the opportunity to meet and interview
   her before she starts although you should exchange letters
   first.

◆ She may have very poor English, at least to begin with.

◆ The hours may not be enough for two full-time working
   parents.

◆ Suits a family of school-age children or where one parent
   works part time.

How to choose

◆ Personal contacts and recommendations are usually the best.

◆ Place adverts in The Lady or in working holiday guides. You
   can also answer adverts placed by au pairs themselves.

◆ An agency may be a good option – addresses of au pair
   agencies are available from The Federation of Recruitment and
   Employment Services (address at back of book).

◆ Other useful addresses are available from The Home Office,
   Immigration and Nationality Department (address at back of
   book).

◆ Send the prospective au pair as much information about your
   family as you can, including how you envisage the
   arrangement to work. Ask for specific information in return.

◆ Take up references, especially if she has au-paired before.
◆ If she has already au-paired, find out how much of her two years remains if she comes from a non-EEC country.

Making it work

◆ Actively help your au pair to make friends. Ensure that she attends English classes. A lonely au pair will be of no use to you or your children.
◆ Make sure she has her own room and some privacy.
◆ Treat her in the same way you would want your own daughter treated in a foreign country.
◆ Make the 'rules' and arrangements clear from the start and stick to them.

FRIENDS AND RELATIVES

If you only need occasional child care this can work well, especially if you can reciprocate by looking after a friend's children in return. You may have a relative who is prepared to look after your children as a favour but beware of using friends in this way, especially if you are paying. You will need to make the arrangement more formal by asking your friend to register as a child minder.

GETTING HELP WITH CHILD CARE

Your employer may pay towards the cost of child care or simply make the choice easier for you. This may be done by providing a workplace nursery or else your employer may buy or subsidise a place in a local day nursery or with a child minder. An employer can provide child care vouchers for their employees which can be used to pay for any legal form of child care. You can find out about child care vouchers from Childcare Vouchers Ltd or Child Care

Cheques (addresses at back of book). You or your employers can also get support and further information from Working For Childcare, Choices in Child Care, Childcare Solutions, and The National Childcare Campaign (addresses at back of book). You may want to start up a working parents group in your place of employment who can work together with your employer to make the whole issue of child care easier. Providing help with child care can attract many women back to the workplace as well as keep the present work force – an attractive proposition for your employer.

If your child has special needs, then social services will pay for your child care. Contact your social worker for further information. If you are on an Employment Training Scheme, then child care should be provided so ask about this when you are offered a place.

THE AFTER-SCHOOL AND HOLIDAY DILEMMA

It is all too easy to imagine that child care will solve itself once your children start school but for many parents the problems just start all over again. As with pre-school care, it is worth planning well ahead, even down to making sure you live in the catchment area of a school which has a good after-hours club. There are alternatives, of course, and you will certainly want to consider all the options, bearing in mind that by now your child will have his own opinions about the sort of care he wants.

Help at home

It is unlikely that you will want to keep on a full time nanny or mother's help once your children are out most of the day. However, you may find someone willing to collect your children and stay with them in your house at the end of each school day. This can prove difficult but you may have more luck finding help for the school holidays when students are likely to be off from college and looking to earn a bit of spare cash.

Child minders

When you choose your child minder for your pre-school child, you may want to plan ahead and use one who also takes in children after school. Some will collect from school while others live a safe distance for your child to walk, especially once he is a little older.

Shared care

If you do not work full time, you may be able to team up with another working parent and take turns to collect the children and take them back to your home. This shared care could also be used in the school holidays if you both agree to take leave at different times.

After-school/holiday clubs

Your child may be lucky enough to attend a school with an after-school club and even a holiday club. Some local authorities also provide out of school clubs which take children from a number of local schools. This is often ideal but is dependent on where you live. There may also be a problem with your child getting to the club if it is not located at his own school. However, it may be possible for a group of parents to supervise the walk to the club on a rota basis. You may want to discuss the possibility of a club with your school or local authority or you may be prepared to help set one up. In this case get further information and support from The Kids Clubs Network (Out of School Alliance) or The National Playing Fields Association (addresses at back of book).

Au pairs

These are ideal for full-time working parents of school-age children. Au pairs are restricted to five hours a day of work and this should enable them to take children to and from school, take care of them after school ends and do a little housework in between.

Holidays for children

Activity holidays for unaccompanied children are usually available for those over the age of 8. Some organisations will take younger children. Many companies advertise in daily and Sunday newspapers. Alternatively, contact The British Activity Holiday Association (address at back of book). It can give you a list of holiday companies which have membership of its organisation. Members are inspected and have to comply with a strict code of practice. Anyway, holidays for under-nines have to be registered with social services and others are covered by health and safety regulations. Your child would probably find it easier to go with friends, so get together with other families you know in the same situation.

Home alone

There is no legal age limit stating at what age children can be left alone. However, you are responsible for your own children and would be accused of neglect if they are clearly too young to cope. Most people consider that children of primary school age should not be left alone for any length of time. It may be possible to have a gradual changeover from full care to self care. You could, for example, enlist the help of a neighbour who could pop in occasionally to check that your child is all right. Whatever your child's age, you will want to have very clear rules about safety and emergencies. Your child should have a set procedure for answering the door and telephone and should have an emergency contact. Make sure he knows how to make a 999 call. Have rules about the use of electrical equipment, having friends back to play and getting home from school. If this is to include cycling, make sure your child takes a cycling proficiency test first. You could also have safe call-ins along the way, making sure he knows where these friends live. Give him a phone charge card, available from BT and programmed to call your work number only. It may be possible to organise a taxi to and from school but you will need to stick to a reliable and reputable firm. This arrangement would clearly need to be organised with great care.

CONTINGENCY PLANS

You must be prepared for all events and that includes your child-minding arrangements breaking down, your child being ill, being ill yourself or getting stuck in traffic on the way home. Have an arrangement to cope with any eventuality. Do, however, try to remain optimistic. Your contingency plans should only be needed on rare occasions. If your normal arrangements are constantly breaking down, you may need to reconsider them.

Prevention is better than panic

Try to choose child care which is reliable. Nursery care is bound to be more reliable than a sickly mother's help who lives two bus rides away. When choosing a child minder, ask if she has her own contingency plan in case she is ill – some minders have arrangements with each other. Encourage your nanny to mix with other nannies as this may prove helpful in emergencies. Keep your children as healthy as you are able, perhaps giving a vitamin C supplement during the winter months. Allow plenty of time for journeys to and from work.

Neat networks

When you are out at work all day, it takes some effort to build up a relationship with neighbours and local friends. Paradoxically, this would be so much easier if you were at home looking after children all day. Be assertive and introduce yourself to neighbours. Keep up contacts you make in antenatal classes or at the clinic. Talk to other parents who use the same nursery or child minders. You could try joining a local branch of the National Childbirth Trust or Parents at Work (national addresses at back of book). Remember that 'networking' works two ways so be prepared to offer your help when it is needed by other busy parents in a temporary crisis. And if another parent has bailed you out recently, do what you can to reciprocate – perhaps by babysitting or having her children to play at a weekend.

Child care breakdown

When you have a sudden breakdown in your arrangements – perhaps your nanny has disappeared or your child minder is ill – you should be prepared with some options to help you out. Would you or your partner be able to take your child to work with you? Is there anyone in your network of friends who can step in at short notice? Are you able to take paid or unpaid leave at a moment's notice? Do you have a local agency who could provide temporary help straight away? Or try a national agency such as Universal Aunts (address at back of book). Keep telephone numbers of such agencies together with numbers of helpful friends and relatives next to the phone.

Ill prepared

You cannot expect your nursery or child minder to take a very sick child, nor would you want them to. It may be that the only person who your child wants when he is feeling so poorly is you or your partner. You and your partner should have discussed such an eventuality with your employers before it happens. After all, few children get through their early years without some sickness. Ask your employer, in advance, if you are able to take paid or unpaid leave at a moment's notice. Do not be tempted to send your child to nursery when he is clearly unwell but on the other hand do not keep him at home with the slightest runny nose (easily done by a guilty parent). Typically, working mothers drag themselves to work when they have terminal flu and the temperature of an oven because they want to 'save' their sick leave for when the children get it. However, do take time off when you are really ill as this will help you to recover more quickly. And do not keep your child off from nursery just because you are at home. When you are unwell, the last thing you want is a toddler bouncing on your sick bed. Save your energy for when they get home at the end of the day. It may be worth returning to work in the summer months so that you have all settled in to the new routine before the coughs and colds season begins.

Unforeseen panic

Prevention is better but it can happen – you are stuck in the middle of a traffic jam half an hour away from your child who needs picking up in one-and-a-half minute's time. The most important thing is not to get tense and panicked. Your nanny, nursery teacher, child minder or school teacher is not going to run off and leave your child on the street to fend for himself. A trained child care worker will also be able to keep your child calm and occupied. You can grovel, apologise and compensate financially later so do not worry. The next important thing is to let your carer know what has happened as soon as possible. It may be better to stop and make a couple of phone calls – one to the carer and one to someone who may be able to help – even if it sets you back a few more minutes. This will help you to calm down, as well as let everyone know what has happened. If being late happens more than once in a short time, be honest and consider whether you are just not allowing enough time for travel.

Gone wrong forever

It may happen that the child care you have arranged breaks down irretrievably – you may just decide that it is unsuitable, or the carer may decide that you or your child are unsuitable! Do not rush into any rash decisions – most child care arrangements will have their teething problems. However, if it really has to end then decide whether it has to be immediate or if you would be prepared to wait until you have something better sorted out. Otherwise you will need to fall back on some of the contingency plans listed above. Sack nannies in a quick no-nonsense manner. Do not beat around the bush or make feeble excuses. Tell her exactly why she/he will have to leave and pay him/her what is due unless she/he has broken his/her contract or done anything illegal.

Using agencies

You can use an agency in an emergency to get temporary help to see you through a problem patch. Or you can use an agency right from the start to employ a nanny or mother's help. An agency will mean an initial financial outlay but is good for speed or for finding specialist nannies (if your child has special needs, for example). They can be useful in larger cities where there are several local papers.

Ask how many nannies they find employment for and make sure they interview them all and get references. If the agency is a member of the Federation of Recruitment and Employment Services, this will ensure a good code of practice.

THE CHILD CARE ROUTINE

The part of the child care routine which you will be involved in is saying goodbye and then saying hello again when you collect your child. Hopefully, you will build up enough trust in your child's carer not to worry about the bit in between. In many ways introducing child care is easier at an early age, at least from your child's point of view, and this may influence when you decide to return to work. However, even a child who has settled in easily as a young baby may go through a clingy phase later. It is certainly worth considering the likely problems at different ages.

Under 3 months

Although your baby will already have built up a close relationship with you, he will not yet have developed a fear of strangers. This is therefore a good age to get into the child care routine. At this stage it is you who will need to get used to leaving him.

3–9 months

Your baby will probably object as you leave the room but this will be short lived as he will be easily distracted. He will form new relationships with ease and so should settle well into a new routine.

9–18 months

This is the stage when babies develop a fear of strangers. However, he will separate from you well if he is being handed over to a familiar adult. It is therefore worth investing some time in settling your child in and allowing him to get to know his carer.

18 months–3 years

If your child has never been left before then he is likely to be quite clingy, at least for the first few times. Your child may make quite a loud objection to being left but check with the carer afterwards – many children settle down quickly once a parent is out of sight. His main fear is that you will not be coming back, so reassure him in simple language. Bear in mind that he will have little concept of time so explain that you are going to work and that you will be back after he has had his lunch, snack or whatever. Leaving something of yours behind can also help – ask him to look after it for you until you return.

3–5 years

Children of this age may still object at the point of leaving but will settle into the routine quickly. You will be able to prepare him for the change much better as verbal explanations will be more easily understood. He will also have developed a greater concept of time and will understand that you are returning. He will be able to talk about his own fears and emotions more readily and you will be able to adopt a goodbye regime which suits you both.

Over 5 years

Few children start school without some experience of being separated from their parents. Usually, they will have had some preparation for starting school which should make the transformation fairly easy. However, do make sure that your child has visited the school and knows all about it well in advance.

DOS AND DON'TS OF SAYING GOODBYE

Do focus on your child. Until he is two, he will not gain from seeing you greet the carer in a friendly way. He will just interpret this as being ignored.

Explain what is going to happen even to a very young child. Do not just leave your child with no explanation or you will lose his trust. However, do not linger at the nursery or child minder's giving long, detailed explanations – keep it quick and simple.

Prepare your child as best you can by visits to the child minder's or nursery. His first day there should not be the first day he has met his new carer.

If practical, build up the hours he is away from you gradually.

If you are to employ a nanny, have at least one day all together before you go back to work. Or perhaps the new nanny would be prepared to pop in on a weekend beforehand.

Take into account your child's age and personality when deciding how to leave. Some children like to be settled in; some children are better if you leave quickly.

Never pretend you are staying and then leave when your child is not looking. He is more likely to be clingy the next time.

Try not to show your own anxiety – your child will respond to this.

Never be clingy yourself – if your child settles do not linger, just give a quick no-nonsense goodbye.

Discuss any separation difficulties with the nursery staff or child minder and take their advice. They will know how your child behaves once you have gone.

Do linger outside, unseen, if you need reassuring that your child really is all right once you have gone. You could also arrange to telephone at a mutually convenient time if this will help to reduce your anxiety.

Do let babies and toddlers have a special toy or comforter if this helps but discuss it with his carer first. If he has an irreplaceable toy, buy an identical one in case of loss.

Do leave your toddler with something of yours if it helps him to learn that you will return.

Tell your child what you will both be doing when you get back – again, this gives him a sense of your return.

If your child is still going through a clingy phase, keep him busy and distracted until you get to the nursery. Clingy behaviour which starts at breakfast can make you both very tense.

Sometimes, your child finds the goodbye much easier if someone else drops him off. See if your partner or a friend can help out and take this as a sign that you are displaying your anxiety or guilt.

Do not use bribery or threats to help your child settle. However, you can talk about something good that you will be doing later – even if it is just having a cuddle and a story.

Give it time. To start with, many children object to being left or are genuinely anxious about the change. Stick to your goodbye routine and he will soon settle down.

Do not apologise when you drop your child off. He will pick up your very negative attitude towards his care.

Discuss the arrangement quite openly with your children. A book can be a useful staring point and The National Childminding Association (address at back of book) suggests some useful stories.

Do encourage your child to talk about his day and the people he is with. Show an interest in what he has been doing

Ask your carer what your child particularly enjoys doing there, so you can talk about the positive aspects of his day.

DOS AND DON'TS OF SAYING HELLO

You will enjoy it most when your child is obviously happy and settled but then rushes over to greet you when he sees you are there.

Your child may look up and smile but finish the task he is doing before he greets you properly. Do not show any disappointment, this just shows how secure and adjusted he is.

If your child ignores you completely, he may be punishing you for leaving him. However, make sure that you show your pleasure in seeing him again and eventually he will greet you more warmly. Do not ignore him and start chatting to his carer or you will not be available when he is ready to say 'Hello'.

Your child may burst into tears of relief when he sees you. Although he is clearly still in the process of settling into a new situation, do not get emotional yourself or start apologising. Just show that you understand and give your child the extra affection he needs.

Make sure that you are ready to greet your child. This will mean trying to unwind as much as possible on the way back from work. When you get in, give your child your undivided attention for at least a few minutes even if you cannot normally settle properly until the dinner is started or you have opened the post.

Some children need time to themselves before they are ready to tell you all about their day. Respect this and try to accommodate yourself to their needs at this time.

WHAT DOES MUMMY DO ALL DAY?

It helps children to be able to visualise their parents in the work place. This is clearly helped by visits there. The following children have never or rarely visited their mother's place of work. They answered . . .

'Speaks on the phone, hoovers and goes to the office.'
> Sarah (5) daughter of an administrative officer.

'Drives in the car. It's red.'
> Anna (3½), daughter of an accountant.

Further questioning revealed that Anna sees her mother leave in the car and arrive back in it at the end of the day. She could only seem to picture her in the car.

'Works at the clinic. Sometimes goes to aerobics and sometimes goes shopping.'
> Adrian (6), son of a receptionist at a health centre.

'Works in an office doing number work. I can write my numbers. My mum's got a calculator at home. I can work it.'
> Morgan (4), son of an accountant.

The following children were more familiar with their mothers' work surroundings and could certainly visualise them there.

'I'm glad my mum helps children. I went with her to see a little boy who could not learn properly. It made him happy and laugh. I'm pleased my mum does that job.'
> Jenny (8), daughter of a home teacher.

'My mum's got a big desk and a chair which goes round and round. You can phone Daddy on her phone.'
> Guy (5), son of a hospital administrator.

'I had Ribena in my mum's clinic. She has toys there and plays with children who can't say things properly.'
> Jessica (5), daughter of a speech therapist.

'My mum tells her shop what to sell. I go in and look at the pretty clothes. I would like a golden handbag.'
> Meg (7), daughter of a fashion buyer.

TIME TIPS

◆ Mark on the map the area within which you could reasonably look for child care. A very long journey at the beginning of the day suits few parents.

◆ You might consider a bus rather than a car journey. This gives you time to talk, read or sing with your child without the stresses and distractions of driving.

◆ When interviewing nannies or mother's helps, eliminate some on the telephone. If you know within two minutes of the interview that she/he is unsuitable, cut the interview short. There is no need to go through the whole procedure if you are absolutely sure that she/he is unsuitable.

◆ Casual chats to a possible carer may seem like time wasting but can reveal a lot. A child minder off guard may tell you more than she realises about her attitude.

◆ If you end up with a long list of possible nurseries or child minders, you visit half and ask your partner to visit the other half. Only visit the best of the bunch together.

◆ Leave plenty of time in the morning to say goodbye to your child. A child who feels rushed may also feel unsettled. You may inadvertently be giving the message that you cannot wait to get rid of him.

◆ Have a box by the door in which to put lunch boxes, coats and so on as you get ready. Then you will not leave anything behind, lying on the hall floor.

◆ Keep a list of what equipment and nappies you have left with the child minder. Then you will know when stock-up time is approaching.

◆ If you have to take some items to the child minder/nursery each day, leave a week's supply in the back of the car.

◆ Make the weekend start on Friday. Stop off at the takeaway and then you can have the whole evening together.

FIVE-MINUTE CHECKLIST:
CAN YOU SHARE YOUR CHILD?

You will have mixed feelings when your child forms a good relationship with his carer. On the one hand you will be relieved and delighted that your child is happy and settled. On the other hand, you may worry that you are being replaced as a parent, especially when the inevitable happens and your child calls her 'mum'! You know deep down that your relationship is special and that your child is benefiting from liaising with other adults. But how do you really feel? Check that you have adjusted to shared care by asking yourself these questions:

◆ YOUR CHILD DRAWS A PICTURE OF YOUR FAMILY WHICH INCLUDES HIS CARER. DO YOU POINT OUT STRAIGHT AWAY THAT SHE IS NOT PART OF THE FAMILY?

◆ YOU FIND OUT THAT YOUR CHILD'S CARER HAS A PET NAME FOR HIM. DO YOU ASK HER NEVER TO USE IT AGAIN?

◆ YOUR CHILD SPENDS ALL EVENING TALKING ABOUT HOW WONDERFUL HIS CARER IS. DO YOU FEEL JEALOUS?

◆ YOUR CHILD ACCIDENTLY CALLS YOU BY HIS CARER'S NAME. DO YOU FEEL PUT OUT?

◆ YOUR CHILD IS INVOLVED WITH HIS CARER WHEN YOU GO TO COLLECT HIM OR GET HOME FROM WORK. HE DOES NOT RUSH OVER TO GREET YOU. DO YOU FEEL GUILTY AND BLAME YOURSELF?

◆ ARE YOU SECRETLY PLEASED WHEN YOUR CHILD CLINGS ON TO YOU AS YOU LEAVE? DOES IT MAKE YOU FEEL NEEDED?

◆ DO YOU MAKE A POINT OF SPENDING THE WEEKENDS DOING THINGS WHICH YOUR CHILD'S CARER COULD NOT POSSIBLY DO?

◆ DO YOU EVER POINT OUT HIS CARER'S FAULTS TO YOUR CHILD OR DISCUSS THEM IN FRONT OF HIM?

◆ YOUR CHILD GOES TO THE NANNY WITH A CUT KNEE INSTEAD OF YOU. DO YOU BURST INTO TEARS?

◆ DO YOU SECRETLY WISH THAT YOU COULD SPEND 24 HOURS A DAY WITH YOUR CHILD?

Acknowledge your feelings and talk to other parents about theirs. Many parents feel a kind of jealousy towards the carer to start with and this is often a symptom of guilt. Once you all settle into the new routine and you realise that you are the most important person in your child's life, you should get these feelings into perspective.

CHAPTER FOUR

Five Minutes With Your Baby

'People who say they sleep like a baby, usually don't have one.'

Leo J. Burke

In many ways, this is one of the most difficult stages of parenthood. If it is your first baby, your life will suddenly be thrown into turmoil and the emotional impact of caring for someone else will be dramatic. Before baby, you may have been a highly organised person, managing your time to good effect. Suddenly, you have to be completely adaptable and flexible as you just do not know when your baby is going to need you. The rewards will seem endless but so will the worries and it is easy to spend many a 'five minutes' just worrying about whether you are doing well as a new parent. If you return to work during the first few months after the birth, you will probably experience an even greater emotional upheaval even though, from your baby's point of view, this may be the easiest time to cope with separating from you.

Your baby will need to adapt too, to the rather stricter timetable that returning to work will involve. However, there are some aspects of caring for a baby which make this stage somewhat simpler than looking after a toddler. For a start, babies sleep a lot of the time and secondly, they are not very mobile, at least to begin with. You should, therefore, be able to organise your time around baby's sleeping patterns though you may want to get your baby to adapt her sleep times so that she is awake when you are home from work.

In the early stages, five minutes is a very meaningful time slot.

Babies have short bursts of concentration and so short bursts of parenting suit this stage of development. It is very easy to over-stimulate a very young baby, causing obvious distress. Babies not only need more sleep, they also need time to themselves just to look at a mobile or the leaves blowing in the wind, without the distraction of someone endlessly singing 'Baa baa black sheep'. You will probably develop some of your own games and activities to share from an early stage. Here we look at these special activities, others which your baby can do while you are doing something else alongside her, and further games which enable you to play an essential role in her development.

FIVE MINUTES GRABBED

Feeding time

Whether you are breast or bottle feeding, this is going to be a close and intimate time between you and your baby. You therefore do not want to be rushed or interrupted. If you feel stressed or have hurried straight home from work to feed her, put on a little relaxing music, make yourself a refreshing drink and just enjoy this special time. After about four months, your baby will start to enjoy some solid food. As soon as she can sit in a high chair, use it so that she can be with the rest of the family at meal times. But do not try to eat your meal and feed a baby just starting on solids at the same time. You may want to feed her first and then put some stick-on toys on to the table of her high chair. Meal times can be a social occasion right from the start so enjoy a 'chat' together at this time. Reluctant feeders can be helped by little games – the spoon can be a train chugging towards the tunnel (baby's mouth). Or you might like to sing your way through – 'this is the way we eat our banana', and so on.

Bath time

New babies often hate being undressed and bathed so the aim will simply be to wash your baby, reassure her and get her used to it. If you have been working, this will not be the most rewarding activity to come home to so if it can be delegated, do so. However, after two or three months, bath time becomes a pleasurable experience for most babies and parents. By six months, your baby will even be babbling and kicking her legs in excitement when she hears the water running. At this stage, you might want to ensure that it is you doing the bathing as the experience will now be fun for both of you. Once your baby can sit up in the bath, have a box of floating toys to hand. Plastic containers, empty plastic bottles and the toy tea set are ideal. Have a pot of bubbles nearby and make the bath bubbly so you can hide things in your hand under a pile of soapy bubbles. See if your child can blow the bubbles off and see what you are holding. Get in with your baby occasionally, although this is no substitute for a real wallow on your own, which you will need from time to time.

Changing time

Very young babies do not like being undressed or having their nappy changed so distract them with a mobile hanging over the changing area and do the job quickly. However, for older babies, this is a good time for tickling games, 'Round and round the garden' or 'Peek-a-bo'. It is an excellent time for babbling together as well as doing some more physical games. Without the restriction of her nappy, your baby might like to do some 'gym' with you. Clap her feet together in front of her face, wrap her in a towel and roll her over or jump her up and down on your knee.

Bed time

This is a time for you both to unwind. Sometimes you will want to drag this part of the day out to enjoy your baby to the last minute and sometimes you cannot wait until she is asleep. Stick to the routine whatever your mood and try to unwind yourself at this time. Ideal activities are gentle songs, stories and, of course, cuddles. If you have a routine, your baby will know it is time to settle down. Some babies are happy to chat and play in their cots until they drop off. You will be able to judge whether to put interesting things in the cot or whether they merely distract her.

Play time

As your baby matures, she will start to have many more alert periods during the day. You should be able to work out when your baby is likely to be responsive to playing with you. Do not try and play with a tired or hungry baby – she will soon let you know if she is not interested. She will also let you know when she has had enough, so look out for tell-tale body language as well as responding to cries and whimpers. Babies turn their heads away when they have had enough or when they are being over-stimulated. Make sure you look into your baby's eyes when you chat or play, though you should find this comes quite naturally.

0–4 months Chatting and singing are the best 'games' at this stage. Babies love faces so give her a change from yours by making teddy and rabbit do the talking.

4–7 months Peek-a-bo with yourself or a pop-up toy. A wooden spoon with a face drawn on popping out of a cardboard tube is ideal. Play repetitive games such as 'Round and round the garden' and 'This little piggy'. Sit in front of the mirror together and make faces. Roll a ball to each other.

7–12 months Your baby will love putting things in and out of containers so keep a box of interesting items handy. Tip them out and talk about them as your baby puts them back. Crawl around the room together going behind furniture and through cardboard box tunnels. Look at books or photos of the family for a quiet five minutes.

FIVE MINUTES SHARED

There are times when your baby will get your undivided attention and other times when she will be quite happy to watch you as long as you chat to her and involve her as she gets older.

If you are working in the kitchen, make sure your baby is at an appropriate height to see what you are doing. If it is safe to do so, put her chair up on the side or table. However, if her movements can jog the chair along, play safe and keep it on the floor. From the age of four or five months, your baby might enjoy being hung from the kitchen doorway in a baby bouncer. And from six or seven months, she might like sitting in a baby walker. Make sure you chat as you work and give your child similar objects to yours, such as a saucepan and wooden spoon. Have a mobile or string of objects to swipe at in each room, together with a box of toys or interesting objects for her to handle once she is old enough. As soon as your baby can pull up to stand or toddle along, she can have her own duster or cloth. Switching a music tape on may distract her when you have to pop into another room to fetch something.

You may have shared time when you are driving to and from nursery or the child minder; your baby will not have your full attention but will enjoy listening to your voice. Have toys to play with on a string as you will not be able to retrieve dropped items while driving.

FIVE MINUTE GAMES

Even if your time with your baby is restricted by work, you will play an essential role in helping her to learn and develop.

Looking games

To begin with, your baby will only be able to see about 10 inches in front of her face. The main thing to look at is therefore your face. Make your face even more interesting by smiling and chatting. Try looking at pictures of faces. Put her chair in front of the mirror or else something that moves, whether it is a mobile or the washing blowing on the line. From about four months, play 'Peek-a-bo' not only with yourself but by popping toys up from behind a cushion. You will be helping your child to learn that things continue to exist even when she cannot see them. Your baby will watch her hands in front of her face and will gradually learn that they are part of her and she can make them do things. At this stage, you can place things into your baby's hands for her to watch. Also, try finger games such as 'This little piggy' to encourage your baby to be aware of her hands and to look at them.

Listening games

At birth, a baby's hearing is almost as acute as an adult's and it is not long before it is even better. However, your baby needs practice to develop her listening skills and you can help. To start with, she will show a preference for human voices, particularly yours, which she will recognise after only days. Your baby will not like sudden loud noises but will enjoy soft music and gentle rattles. Fill containers with a variety of objects so that your baby can listen to new noises each time you play. Start to shake them to the side of your baby so that she has practice locating a noise and turning towards it. Once your baby is crawling, hide something noisy, such as a ticking clock, under a box for her to crawl and find. From about 10 months, your baby will enjoy making her own noises so have a 'band' together, with wooden spoons and biscuit tins or 'chimes' made of spoons tied together.

Touching and holding games

Very young babies spend a lot of time lying down, so try laying her on different textures – a sheepskin, duvet or blanket. Later, when she can lie on her tummy and lift her head up (about four or five months), try a touch blanket which you can buy or make by attaching different materials and objects to a blanket or quilt. Babies are born with a grasp reflex which they retain for some months, so place different textured objects into your baby's hand for her to feel. Later she will hold an object more readily and may even look at what she is holding. She will learn that it is her causing the rattle to make a sound when she moves her arm. At this stage she will not pick up the objects herself but will swipe at anything hanging within reach. So tie a string of objects above her cot or mat. Once she starts to get hold of them, she is ready to pick things up for herself, so make sure there are things within reach for her to grab. However, to start with your baby will find it difficult to let go of the item. So put your hand underneath and give a gentle tug, gradually encouraging her to do the giving. Make the letting go rewarding for her by doing something exciting with the item, such as banging it on something or putting it on your head.

Talking games

Talk to your baby right from the start – she will respond to the up and down pattern of your voice long before she understands individual words. By about four months your baby will start 'cooing' with open vowel sounds and then real babbling will start at about six or seven months. At this stage, talk or babble back to your baby, leaving time for your baby to 'reply'. She will soon learn that talking involves taking turns. Sing repetitive songs or rhymes to your child and then start to leave the last bit off 'We all fall . . .' or 'Tickle you under . . .'. Your baby will start to vocalise in anticipation and before long will be attempting the word. Start looking at books together from at least nine months. If you always make this a relaxed and pleasurable experience for you both, your baby will soon develop a love of books and stories. Always talk about the things your baby is doing so that she learns to associate your words with the things around her. She will understand many words by nine months and should start to use words soon after her first birthday.

BABY WATCH

Before your baby can talk, she will communicate her needs and emotions by crying and using body language. You will tune into many of these signals quite unconsciously and soon know whether your baby is crying with hunger, pain, frustration or tiredness. You will notice her kick her legs and wave her arms about in excitement and turn her head away when she has had enough. She will greet you with excited limb movements and smiles and from about nine months will also use learnt signals, such as waving. Her facial expressions will indicate a whole range of emotions – excitement, distress, pleasure, pain, curiosity, boredom, tiredness and contentment. You will also become familiar with her routine, knowing when she is most likely to need a sleep or a feed. You will become aware of her alert times when you can both enjoy a chat or a play.

If your work hours are flexible or if you are caring for your child at home, you will be able to fit your routine around your baby's so that you are available to play when she is most alert. However, you may need to manipulate your child's routine so that her alert times coincide with the times when you are going to be with her. So, note if your baby is sleepy after a bath, in which case you may want to leave this until the end of the day or else arrange for her to be bathed when you are out. If you want her to have her sleep times while you are out, you may have to keep her awake at 'your time' in whatever way you can until she settles into a new routine. If you are returning to work while your child is very young, you will want to establish a working routine for her before you return. This may involve starting to wake her up earlier or putting her down for a rest at a different time. If you start work with a reasonably workable routine already established, it will make life easier for both of you at a potentially difficult time.

Do not be surprised if your baby does not always greet you with excitement and a big smile after a day away. She may even look away to start with but within minutes you will get the greeting you deserve. At this stage, you need to be able to read your baby's feelings. Some of this will come quite naturally but it also helps to make yourself aware of your baby's moods and body language. This will help you see things from your baby's point of view so you do not just rush in excitedly hoping for a quick rough and tumble. This will only upset a tired or grumpy baby and in this instance a reassuring cuddle will be more rewarding for both of you. Similarly, be prepared for a rough and tumble if that is what your baby needs, even though you are weary and would rather just sit and hold her on your knee. After all, it is only for five minutes, which is a long time for a baby. Then you can slowly change the activity to suit you both.

FIVE-MINUTE EQUIPMENT

Buy equipment that will save you time or make it easier for you to do two things at once. Do not buy anything that you will use once and then put up in the loft. The best way to predict what you will need is to ask experienced friends what equipment they find invaluable or otherwise. Apart from the essential cot, pushchair and so on, you might consider buying the following:

Baby sling   All babies love this and it keeps your hands free to do other things while your baby sleeps or listens to you talking. A sling is not suitable for people with bad backs. Beware of using it for your baby's sleep times so that she never gets used to being put down in her cot.

Baby bouncer   This can be hung from a door frame for babies from about four or five months. Not all babies take to this so try him in a friend's bouncer first.

Baby walker   From about seven months, your baby will sit in one and will soon learn to propel herself along. Toys can be put on a table in front of the walker. A baby walker is not suitable for children living in small flats and it can make your baby instantly mobile so you need to be very safety conscious. Many parents describe it as their best buy.

Baby relax chair   Not really necessary if you have a portable baby car seat.

Baby intercom   Stops you having to go up and down stairs to check your baby every few minutes. Buy one which is portable enough for you to take out into the garden with you.

Storage boxes   Or anything which will enable you to keep a few toys in each room. Makes tidying up easy – even for a small child

– and stops you running up and down stairs to find something for your baby to play with.

Toys   You will not need a lot of toys at this stage but do collect together anything interesting for your child to play with, provided it is clean and safe. Start with mobiles and move on to things for your child to hold, particularly if they make a noise. A baby gym – a frame with interesting things hanging from it – can be bought or made. Buy interesting objects to bang together at this stage, but which can be used in a more sophisticated way at a later stage – bricks, for example.

Liquidiser or food processor   When you make a meal which would be suitable for your baby, make extra, liquidise it and freeze the portions you are not going to use straight away. For a young baby just starting to eat solid foods, use ice-cube trays to freeze small amounts at a time.

Breast Pump   If you decide to express milk because you are at work for part of the day, you may choose to buy a breast pump. Remember that many women successfully express by hand but choose a method which suits you.

BREAST FEEDING FOR WORKING MOTHERS

Returning to work does not necessarily mean giving up breast feeding altogether. Depending on the hours you work and whether you can see your baby during breaks, you may be able to continue with full-time breast feeding. Otherwise, expressing your milk means that your baby can continue with full-time breast milk even though some of it will be given in bottles. Some mothers will decide not to continue with breast feeding and there is no need to feel guilty about this. After all, it is those first few days of breast feeding which matter the most as your baby will be getting the valuable colostrum from you. Whatever your decision, do take the following factors into consideration as you plan your return to work.

◆ Do have an open mind. If your baby or you are having difficulty with breast feeding or if you are struggling to keep up your milk supply, reconsider your initial decision.

◆ Do start expressing milk and introducing your baby to the bottle before returning to work. You should establish a workable routine in advance.

◆ Do start to build up a supply of frozen breast milk about two weeks before returning to work.

◆ Do try to return to work towards the end of a week so that you quickly have a weekend to regain your strength and re-evaluate your feeding routine.

◆ Do express at work but discuss the details with your employers or supervisors first. You also need to consider where you will store the expressed milk. A cool box is one option.

◆ Do store breast milk in the fridge for up to five hours, in a freezer compartment for up to two weeks and in a deep freeze for up to four months.

◆ Do take advice on what sort of breast pump to use. This is usually easier and quicker than expressing by hand.

◆ Do talk to other working mothers, perhaps through a local branch of the National Childbirth Trust or La Leche League (addresses at back of book).

◆ Do contact these organisations if you would like advice from a breast-feeding counsellor. Or ask for their leaflets on working and breast feeding.

◆ Do remember that your health visitor is another source of information and advice.

◆ Do try to overcome any difficulties your baby may have in accepting a bottle. Try different teats or breast feed with an adapted nipple shield.

◆ Do remind yourself of the benefits of breast feeding and keep it as the relaxed and intimate time it should be.

◆ Do express the night feeds so that these can be shared with your partner.

◆ Do remember that breast feeding can make you tired.

◆ Do remember to keep fit and have a healthy diet while breast feeding.

TIME TIPS

◆ Do not reject commercial baby food, which often has added vitamins.

◆ Freeze home-cooked liquidised food in the quantities your baby needs. Ice-cube trays or plastic egg boxes may be useful for this.

◆ Wear a thin dressing gown or overalls over the top of your work clothes while you get baby ready. To get the sour smell of baby's posset off your shoulder, dab with a damp cloth dipped in some bicarbonate of soda.

◆ Bath time does not have to be in the evening. The morning may suit your routine better.

◆ Get your baby used to being alone for five minutes in his cot when he wakes up. You can then do your jobs and give him your full attention when you do go in.

◆ Keep two bags of nappy-changing equipment, one upstairs and one downstairs. The downstairs bag can also be grabbed quickly when you go out.

◆ Choose clothes which make nappy changing easy and which will not need ironing.

◆ Express milk when you are relaxed and not when you feel rushed. This will make it easier and therefore quicker.

◆ Choose a car/baby seat that you can carry around with you. Your baby will be happy to be taken around the house with you as you load the washing machine and so on.

◆ Get everything you may need for the night feed and change ready the night before. This can include a flask of tea for you.

FIVE-MINUTE CHECKLIST: HAVE YOU ACHIEVED THE BABY BALANCE?

◆ DO YOU KNOW FIVE QUICK, EASY AND UNSTRESSFUL WAYS TO ENTERTAIN YOUR BABY WHEN YOU ARE TOO TIRED TO THINK?

◆ DOES YOUR BABY HAVE A SPECIAL TOY, BLANKET, DUMMY OR THUMB FOR COMFORT WHEN YOU ARE NOT THERE OR TO HELP HER SETTLE AT NIGHT?

◆ HAVE YOU IDENTIFIED A TIME WHEN YOUR BABY IS MORE LIKELY TO BE GRUMPY OR AGITATED? IF SO, HAVE YOU DEVELOPED A REGIME FOR DEALING WITH THIS? (MAYBE BY JUST GOING OUT FOR A LONG WALK.)

◆ DO YOU FIND YOURSELF CONSTANTLY RUNNING ABOUT THE HOUSE SEARCHING FOR FAVOURITE TOYS OR DO YOU KEEP A FEW ITEMS IN EACH ROOM?

◆ DO YOU CATCH YOURSELF CHATTING TO YOUR BABY EVEN WHEN SHE IS ASLEEP, SHOWING THAT YOU ARE NEVER TOO DISTRACTED TO RELATE WELL TO YOUR CHILD?

◆ BABIES LEARN THROUGH EXPERIENCE SO DO YOU LET YOUR BABY MAKE DISCOVERIES BY HERSELF WHEN SHE PLAYS?

◆ HAVE YOU LET YOUR BABY OVERDOSE ON THE BABY SLING SO THAT IT IS IMPOSSIBLE TO PUT HER DOWN TO SLEEP ON HER OWN?

◆ CAN YOU SWITCH OFF WHEN YOU FEED YOUR BABY ENSURING THAT THIS IS A TIME TO RELAX AND NOT JUST ANOTHER JOB TO BE DONE?

◆ DO YOU MAKE THE MOST OF YOUR BABY'S SLEEP TIMES?

◆ DO YOU ALLOW YOURSELF SOME TIME ON YOUR OWN AWAY FROM BOTH WORK AND BABIES AT LEAST ONCE A WEEK?

CHAPTER FIVE

Five Minutes With Your Toddler

'Whoever said caring for a toddler was easy successfully stopped a stampeding elephant by putting up a give way sign.'

Sara Welch

Having an active toddler in the house is both delightful and rewarding. However, he will take up a great deal of your physical and mental energy. He will want to do things for himself, yet will need watching all the time. His new found independence and determination will help him learn and develop but will lead to temper tantrums too. His moods will be harder to predict and his demands on your time will seem never ending. He will now really start to enjoy the company of other children and adults and working parents will start to see the benefits for him of shared care. Toddlers going to a nursery or child minder will begin to develop good social and self-help skills and often very good communication skills as well. Toddlers still benefit from short bursts of learning as their concentration spans will be fairly short. So five or ten minutes looking at a story together is often more valuable than an hour in front of the video when your toddler is barely paying attention at all.

FIVE MINUTES GRABBED

Your toddler will want to help you and do things for himself. At this stage, it may be far easier to do it all yourself but try not to fall into this trap. Despite the possibility of toddler frustration and tantrums, now is the time to set an early trend of everyone joining in with the daily chores. Eventually, he really will be able to help and if this has already been part of his routine, he will not expect you to do everything for him.

Meal times

Give your child his own job – laying the table or even just putting out the spoons. After the meal, he can help put the plates next to the sink or in the dishwasher and he can wipe the table. Set a pattern of having meal times together where you eat and chat without the background noise of the TV or radio.

Bath time

Your toddler will find undressing easier than dressing, and pyjamas easier than day clothes. So bath time is a good chance to encourage dressing skills. You should never leave your toddler unattended, even in a shallow bath, so stay and supervise the water play as well as the washing. Let your toddler wash himself as far as possible and chat about body parts as it is done. Washing a doll in the bath can enhance this learning experience.

Bedtime

Make sure you have a predictable routine for settling your child down for the night. Hopefully, this will include reading a story or quietly looking at a book together. Your child's attention span will be fairly short so you may not want to stick to the 'script' as you read. You will also want to make it an activity your child can actively participate in, so let him comment on the pictures and ask him about the story as you go along.

Other times

Have a few activities up your sleeve which need no preparation, for when you find you can grab an unexpected five minutes together.

Singing For boisterous times, try action songs such as 'Heads, shoulders, knees and toes', 'I'm a little teapot' or 'Row, row, row the boat'.

Easy I-spy A good game to play on the way to nursery as well as at home. Give easy clues to start with such as 'I spy something that barks and has a tail'. If your child finds this hard, just play a fetching game asking him to find things around the room.

Copy Cats Your toddler will enjoy copying your actions and the sillier the better. So crawl round and round the chair or put the cushion on your head.

Mini-gym All toddlers love being swung round, tickled or just having a rough and tumble. Try bicycling your child's legs while he lies on his back. Or lie him on his front and raise his legs up, like in a wheelbarrow race. Cross his arms over his tummy and then stretch them out wide again. Or roll sideways along the floor together.

FIVE MINUTES SHARED

Inevitably, you will have times when your toddler demands your attention while you are cooking a meal or finishing some other task. It is worth having some activities to hand which your toddler can do with only half your attention on him.

Table games

Keep a basket of activities to hand which need little supervision. Colouring, threading, books and story or song tapes are ideal. Change the items frequently so that your toddler never knows what he is going to find in his basket.

Mini-mums

Your toddler will want to copy what you are doing. So if you are writing, give him paper and pencils and if you are cleaning, give him a duster.

Run-around games

Sometimes you can be busy and organise easy run-around games at the same time. Try hunt the thimble – it does not have to be a thimble, a favourite snack may be more rewarding to search for. You can also get your active toddler fetching and carrying for you.

Sitting games

Sitting in front of the television or video can keep a toddler occupied for a long time. But it is not surprising that parents feel guilty if a toddler watches too much TV. After all, it is difficult to assess whether your child is really listening and paying attention. Some programmes are more useful than others, especially if they require some active participation from your toddler. Try to choose videos or TV programmes which encourage your child to do actions or sing along. Do not be afraid of the off switch but have something else ready to attract your child's interest. Maybe a bag full of different objects so he can put his hand in and guess what is inside. Puzzles, bricks and picture-matching games make good alternative activities.

FIVE-MINUTE GAMES

When you can give your child your undivided attention, you may try completely different activities to those designed to keep him occupied while you get on. You will want to join in and you may even risk more messy activities, but do not underestimate the time needed to clear up. Some games will help your child with social and communication skills while others will be good for physical development or manipulation. Your child should and will learn and develop new skills without even trying. The emphasis should be on fun – for both of you.

Less mess

Toddlers love messy games but you need to be aware of your own time limitations when it comes to clearing up. Do painting, glue-ing and the like outside whenever possible. Otherwise cover your floor, table and child. Old shirts make ideal overalls for your child. Old shoes and socks are also a good idea as paint tends to splash downwards. Mix a little washing-up liquid with the paint to make it easier to wash off afterwards and only choose water-soluble, non-toxic paints. Toddlers love water play and a bowl of soapy water outside makes a lovely game. However, if your child goes to a nursery and experiences a lot of sand and water play as well as painting, do not feel that you have to provide it at home. Be realistic about what you can manage in the time available.

Physical games

Try ball throwing – hang a hoop from a tree and see if your tod-dler can throw the ball through it. If catching a ball is difficult, start with a bean bag as this is easier to grip. Make an obstacle course in the garden or even in the lounge. Make a tricycle course and see if your child can pedal in and out of some old plastic bot-tles filled with sand. Take your child swimming but go with a friend so you can take it in turns to have a good swim yourselves.

Manipulation

Try finger rhymes such as 'Incy wincy spider', 'Tommy thumb' and 'Two fat gentlemen met in the lane'. Play 'Pick a straw' with a packet of coloured straws which you throw into a heap. Then take turns to see if you can pick one up without moving the rest. Try easy threading games, perhaps threading cardboard tubes to start with and gradually moving on to cotton reels or dried macaroni.

Communication

Play puppets (faces drawn on paper bags will do) and shops. These are good games to ensure that you both get a chance to do the talking. Play hiding, getting yourselves in, on and under big cardboard boxes – a good game for using those position words (prepositions). Look at books together, taking it in turns to tell the story. Choose stories with repetitive lines such as 'You can't catch me, I'm the gingerbread man' or 'Who's been sleeping in *my* bed?' Encourage your child to join in.

Imagination

Never throw away any old clothes as these are great for dressing-up games. Use play dough, a plastic tea set and teddies and dolls for a tea party or picnic. Make cardboard boxes be anything you want from a car to a shop counter, from a bus to a snail's shell. Take your child's lead, letting him decide what the box could be. Turn everyday activities into imaginative games, so that, for instance, tea time could be a game of cafés.

FIVE MINUTES TO RELAX

Make sure you have at least five minutes to relax whenever you need it. This will involve making the most of your toddler's nap times or early nights. You also need to make the most of your partner and take up any offers of help you get. Remember that time spent with your child does not always have to be physically or mentally demanding. Nor do you have to be constantly entertaining and educating your child. If he is happily playing on his own, enjoy the chance to get on or to put your feet up. And remember there is still value in lying on the couch, listening to a tape and having a cuddle with him.

FIVE-MINUTE SHOPPING: WHAT TO BUY FOR YOUR TODDLER

Once your child is running around, sleeping in a bed and eating the same meals as you, you will need very little baby equipment. You may, however, want to buy some toys and play equipment. You may plan to make some of the soft toys, cook endless supplies of play dough and use all the leftover wood to make a cooker or doll's house. But do be realistic, especially if you are a working parent. Your child does not need a bottomless pit of toys and it is all too easy to waste money on a novelty item which your child plays with maybe only once or twice. So when you choose toys for your child, consider the following:·

♦ Do not buy on impulse or from guilt.
♦ Do not respond to your child's impulse when he spots something in a shop. But do take note of what he likes playing with at friends' houses.
♦ Choose toys which have educational value by all means, but make sure they are fun too.
♦ Choose toys which will last. A puzzle that your child can do easily may soon be discarded but something like building bricks which can be used at different ages in different ways have enormous value.
♦ Choose some toys which are good for sharing, particularly if you have more than one child.
♦ Choose some toys with an emotional value. A special teddy can be a comfort to a young child and help him cope with separation from you.
♦ Choose toys which you can do more than one thing with – a rocking horse is just a rocking horse, whereas Duplo bricks can be anything.
♦ Choose toys which meet the required safety standard – EC standard EN71 or British standard BS 5665.
♦ In your collection it is worth having bricks, books, play dough, miniature people toys, such as play people or Duplo, pencils and crayons, cars and a road mat, board games, such as

picture lotto, puzzles, threading games, a teddy or doll, a tea set, musical 'instruments' or a song tape, scissors and glue, a tricycle and a ball.

TODDLER TRAPS

Toddlers are notoriously delightful one minute and impossible the next. All toddlers go through a stage of temper tantrums and all have gradually to learn good social skills as well as other more practical skills, such as using the toilet. There are some common traps to fall into when dealing with your toddler, particularly when you are working.

◆ Decide on a policy for dealing with temper tantrums and stick to it. Ignore them wherever possible and be consistent with how you deal with inappropriate behaviour.

◆ Do not blame temper tantrums on yourself or the fact that you work. Do not give in to your child out of guilt.

◆ If your child is being cared for by more than one person, make sure that you are consistent with each other on how you manage his behaviour.

◆ If you are trying to help your child with a new skill, such as using the toilet, discuss it with his carer and your partner so that you can have a consistent approach with this too.

◆ Do not do things for your child because it is easier. Let him have a go, giving the minimum help required to curb frustration. Praise all his efforts.

◆ Make sure your child is motivated to do things for himself. Most children naturally are, but if not, have a star chart to reward good efforts.

◆ Have a chart with jobs for all the family. Even young toddlers can have their own special jobs, whether it is making the bed (pulling up the duvet cover and putting pyjamas under the pillow) or wiping the kitchen table after meals.

◆ Try to avoid confrontations and therefore tantrums whenever possible. Start to predict what is likely to cause problems and avoid the situation where possible. Use distraction techniques for getting through problem parts of the day, such as bath time or bed time.

◆ Keep a five-minute basket to hand for when your child needs distracting or occupying. You can collect interesting things, including one or two new items which your child has not seen before. Keep it out of sight for emergencies.

◆ Remember to praise good behaviour as well as ignore the bad. It is easy for children of busy parents to be ignored when they are being good and be given plenty of attention when they are not. Take a look at how much praise you really give.

◆ If you feel yourself getting really hot under the collar, take a breather while your partner or a friend takes over for five minutes.

◆ Remember that 'the terrible twos' is just a stage and things do get better.

THE FIVE-MINUTE ROUTINE

Your toddler may still have a rest in the afternoon and will almost certainly need quiet periods if he is not going to end up tired and grumpy by early evening.

◆ If you come home from work to a tired toddler, discuss rest times with his carer.

◆ Similarly, if your toddler is awake until late evening because of a long daytime sleep, alter his routine. You need some time to yourself at the end of the day.

◆ Mornings can be rushed with unpredicatable toddlers who want to do everything themselves. Get everything ready the night before and allow plenty of time.

◆ Be firm about night waking, which can re-emerge at this stage. You need your sleep too, so settle your child down quickly and silently. Be boring rather than worth waking up to and give your child a reassuring night light and cuddly toy. Use a star chart to reward a good night's sleep.

◆ Although you will want to be flexible, especially at weekends, remember that toddlers feel secure with a predictable routine. So stick to bed times, waking up times and meal times fairly rigidly.

TIME TIPS

◆ Use a duvet and a fitted bottom sheet so that even a young child can make his own bed.

◆ This is the age when parties start. Keep a stock of suitable cards and presents to avoid wasting time popping to the shops at the last minute.

◆ Toddlers love bubble bath and this has the added advantage of keeping the bath clean and preventing that ring around the sides.

◆ Get into your toddler's bed or pop him into yours for the bed time story. At least you will have your feet up and be relaxing.

◆ The first step to getting your toddler to help with tidying up is to give him a basket and ask him to pick everything up off the floor. This will save time and your back.

◆ Keep a supply of new but cheap toys, even a balloon will do. Get one out when you feel a tantrum coming on but do not reward a tantrum once it has started.

◆ Do not make meal times an issue. Not only can you waste hours trying to get a faddy toddler to eat his spinach but you will create tense meal times which will get longer, more frustrating and more stressful.

◆ Have a simple rule that one game is put away before a new one is taken out.

◆ Colour code your child's toy boxes or better still stick a picture on front of each container to show what should go inside.

◆ If your child is tired and grumpy after a day at the nursery/child minder, give him an early bath. This can relax and revive him.

FIVE-MINUTE CHECKLIST:
WHAT CAN YOUR TODDLER DO?

Which of these things could your toddler help with?

◆ WATERING THE PLANTS IN THE GARDEN.

◆ CLEANING THE CAR.

◆ PUTTING HIS TOYS AWAY.

◆ HANGING HIS COAT UP.

◆ PUTTING HIS CLOTHES AWAY.

◆ PUTTING HIS DIRTY CLOTHES IN THE LAUNDRY BASKET OR NEXT TO THE WASHING MACHINE.

◆ PUTTING PLATES IN THE DISHWASHER/NEXT TO THE SINK.

◆ LAYING THE TABLE.

◆ DUSTING.

◆ MAKING HIS BED.

◆ TIDYING HIS ROOM.

◆ WIPING THE KITCHEN TABLE.

◆ FEEDING ANY PETS.

◆ ENTERTAINING A YOUNGER BROTHER OR SISTER.

◆ UNLOADING THE DISHWASHER/PUTTING CLEAN PLATES AWAY.

Which of these things can your toddler begin to do on his own (with maybe a little help from you)?

◆ GET UNDRESSED.

◆ PUT HIS PYJAMAS ON.

◆ BRUSH HIS TEETH.

◆ Wash and dry his hands.

◆ Wash himself in the bath.

◆ Get his clothes out for the day.

◆ Put his coat on.

◆ Brush his hair.

◆ Pack his bag for the nursery/child minder.

◆ Use the toilet, flush it and wash his hands afterwards.

◆ Blow his own nose.

◆ Eat his dinner with a spoon and fork with minimum mess.

◆ Put on slippers or easy-fasten shoes.

◆ Make simple decisions such as what to wear and what to play.

◆ Take some responsibility for his possessions by looking after them and putting them away.

The answer to the first question is that your toddler can help with all of these to a greater or lesser extent. You may need to arrange your house in such a way that he can help more easily – having shelves within reach, having a suitable hook for his coat, and so on. Obviously he will not be able to help with anything which is potentially dangerous, such as ironing or even putting items inside the washing machine. And he will need help with anything involving breakable items. While you are not looking for perfection, you do not want to create more mess to have to clean up, so watering the indoor plants may be out. The aim of the exercise is to set a trend that everyone helps and to give your child a sense of importance and responsibility. Do not, therefore, criticise his efforts or redo his tasks in front of him. At this stage, give praise for just trying and wait until he is out of sight before making any necessary adjustments.

The answer to the second question is that you should be working towards your toddler doing all of these things independently and giving only the necessary help with any other self-help skills.

At this age, your child enjoys trying to do things for himself although you may need to lend a hand in order to avoid frustration. Of course, these things may take a little longer so make allowances by allocating more time in the morning, when you are getting ready to go out, or at bedtime.

CHAPTER SIX

Five Minutes With Your Child

'Before I got married, I had six theories about bringing up children and no children. Now I have six children and no theories.'

Anon

In the run-up to school and during the school years, your child will gradually become more independent, taking more responsibility for her belongings and her actions. She will still need you for emotional support but practical help will change from, say, helping her get dressed to helping with her homework. As the years go by, your child will seem to need you less and less, relying as much on friends and other adults for relationships and entertainment. However, even in the teenage years your child will need you emotionally and more than she is prepared to admit. You will want to make yourself available for support and advice and just to listen. And you will want to let go. You will have been a successful parent if your child becomes confident in her independent skills but it is all too easy to cling on to the old parental role and do as much as you can for your school-age child or teenager. Just because you no longer have to do her shoes up, and just because she wants to read her own bedtime story, does not mean that you no longer have a role to play. Accept that the role of parent is a changing one and enjoy the new challenges that come as your child matures. It is at this stage that you may take on more work or additional interests outside the family. Although your child is at school during the day, the problems of juggling your time still continue. In fact, you will need to be more organised than ever before.

FIVE MINUTES GRABBED

As your child gets older, she is more likely to be involved in activities outside the home which do not involve you, except perhaps as a taxi service. When your child goes to nursery and then school, you may be able to work longer hours or take on new responsibilities. It can therefore become increasingly difficult to plan your schedule so that you can spend time as a family. Try to grab some time together at least once a day when you are not all rushing off to do something else.

Meal times

Sit round the table and eat meals together, even if you worked late and then stopped off to pick up fish and chips on the way home. Let the whole family decide when would be a good time for the evening meal and stick to it as far as possible. Be inflexible about this. If your child is allowed to grab her plate and sit in front of the TV once, you will have started a trend for separate eating patterns.

After school

You may see your child straight after school or nursery or she may go to an after-school club or child minder's first. Either way, you need to observe your child well, be tuned into her pattern of emotions and have a good deal of sensitivity to her needs. For every child is different. Some children need time with you straight away to pour out all that has happened in your absence or to get any problems off their chest. Other children need time to relax and unwind, sometimes on their own, before wanting any sort of conversation at all. You too may want time on your own right away but, in the long run, you may find it better to fit in with your child's needs and if necessary grab your solitary time later. Remember that spending time with your child can be relaxing. Relaxation and parenting are not mutually exclusive. You do not have to be doing anything educational or exciting, for at the end of the day what your child needs most is someone to listen to her and to show her that she is interesting, loved and cared for. You can do all that with your feet up and a cup of tea in your hand. Show your child that you are on her side as far as problems are concerned; you can be both firm and understanding. Saying 'You're a big girl now, you don't need to worry about that', shows that you don't understand. So listen first and offer practical advice after you have sympathised.

Bedtime

If your child has reading to do from school, you could do it at this time. You can read her a story and she can read you one. This makes reading less like 'homework' and more like fun time together. Stop reading your child a bedtime story when she wants you to stop, which should be well after she has learnt to read fluently by herself. Even school children benefit from a bedtime routine which should be a relaxing time for you both. Encourage your child to get everything ready for the next morning before she goes to bed.

Morning time

For working parents, this is not often a good time to relax together. Get school bags, lunch boxes and work clothes all ready the night before. Make sure your child understands the importance of getting up, getting dressed and not demanding her sports kit at the last moment. Have a list up in the kitchen or bedroom to remind you which day is football, art, dancing, and so on, so you can get the necessary equipment ready the night before. Even a very young child can understand the concept of getting to work on time, letting people down and even losing a job through persistent lateness. If your child suddenly confronts you with an emotional crisis, you will have to defer it until later. But give her a set time when you promise to talk about it and write it down so she knows you will not forget.

FIVE MINUTES SHARED

Taking your child to work

If it is practical, try to arrange for your child to drop in and see you at work and meet some of your colleagues. This will help her understand what you do and she will be able to picture you there. You will soon find out that children have a very positive reaction to their parents' jobs. Your child will most likely be very proud of what you do and if both parents work, she will not grow up with a set view on female and male roles in life. Talk about your work at the end of she day, preferably in a positive way. If your child senses that you are guilty about the hours you work, she may be tempted to use this as emotional blackmail. Far better for your positive approach to work to rub off on her.

Doing homework together

Parental guilt can affect your attitude to homework and you can end up doing a whole project for your child to make up for working. This is clearly illogical so always remind yourself that the purpose of homework is for your child to work on her own and practise what she has learnt. One solution is to sit at the table with your child doing some paper work yourself or even to get your child working in the kitchen while you cook dinner. This way you are available for advice but busy enough for your child to attempt it on her own as far as possible. Younger children are likely to have a reading book and this will require your full attention. You can make this part of your evening routine but stick to what the school sends home. Guilty parents may try to compensate by whisking out flash cards or home reading schemes as soon as their children get home. Stick to the school's advice and use the rest of your time together for less pressurised and more relaxing activities. If your child is having problems with her homework, arrange to discuss it with her teacher. Ask how long your child is expected to work each evening and try to keep to this recommendation.

Shared relaxation

As your child gets older, you may like to involve her in one of your interests, whether it is teaching her to play tennis or doing yoga together. This is as well as time on your own indulging in your hobby, not instead of. Another relaxing shared activity is watching TV. Get involved in a good children's drama series – you may well get as hooked as your child and you can chat about it at other times, even following it up by reading the book of the series together. Some parents enjoy renting out videos of the films they enjoyed as children. You can then have your own cinema in the lounge complete with popcorn and a fizzy drink. You are relaxing, indulging in a bit of nostalgia and still giving your child time and attention.

FIVE-MINUTE GAMES

There may be times when you want to play the sorts of games which will help prepare your child for starting school or which will help her learning skills once she has started. The emphasis is on fun, on having little or no preparation and on lasting for as long or short a time as you have available.

Self-help practice games

To encourage your child to master the art of dressing herself, play dressing-up games with all your old cast-offs. Getting into big items is easier than the correctly sized ones but will give your child confidence to tackle the 'real thing'. Play shoe shops and get your child doing up laces and buckles in a fun, no-rush situation. Keep all your old baby clothes and dress teddy and dolly too. Give your child plastic cutlery and play dough to help her when it comes to cutting up her real dinner.

Listening games

Tell your child a familiar story such as 'The Three Bears' but make some deliberate errors for her to spot. This might be as simple as saying 'Once upon a time there were three goats' or more difficult, such as 'Mummy put the porridge into the two bowls'. As you are making this up as you go along, you can play it anywhere and while you are doing something else, such as driving. Play traffic lights where you shout out 'green' and your children run, 'amber' for walking and 'red' for stopping. Keep adding more things such as 'Run out of petrol' where they have to sit down. Play a version of blind man's buff where your blindfolded child has to find you by the sound of your voice.

Talking games

Play twenty questions but for younger children restrict this to an item in the room or something specific such as an animal. Play 'Just a minute' where you have to talk on a chosen topic for one minute without repeating yourself. Turn the sound down when your child is watching a favourite sport or special event and see if she can do a commentary – not as easy as it sounds. Get your child doing some logical thinking by asking hypothetical questions – 'What would happen if all cars were yellow?' or 'What would happen if people only had one arm each?'

Looking games

Make a simple building out of bricks and see if your child can make an identical one with a matching set of bricks. Now make it more difficult by covering your version up first. Play 'Kim's game' where you put out some objects on a tray. Remove one while your child shuts her eyes and then see if she can work out which one you have taken away. Play a game of treasure hunt by hiding something in the house or garden – you could give clues to help. Or else change something round in one of the rooms and see if your child can work out what is different.

Action games

Play newspaper cricket where the bat is a rolled up newspaper and the ball a balloon or a screwed up piece of paper. Get your child to set up her own obstacle course in the garden and then you both have a go at doing it.

Imaginative games

Play charades – older children can act out a film, book or TV programme while younger children could try acting out a particular job. Get your children and their friends to act out a familiar story or nursery rhyme for you to watch. See how many animals your child can pretend to be. Play story rounds where you start off a story and then your child carries on with the next bit. Keep taking it in turns until the story ends or you run out of time.

Reading and writing games

Tracing, colouring, cutting out and glueing are all useful pre-writing activities. Buy magnetic letters to stick on the fridge – your child can play with them while you are busy or you can make some words for her to copy underneath with matching letters. If you have time to make flash cards, do, but use them in a fun way. Most useful are words to match with things around the house. Your child can then see if she can stick them on to the correct item. Once your child has begun to read and write, involve her in day-to-day activities, such as making a shopping list or seeing who the post is for. Later, she can play pencil and paper games with you, such as consequences or hangman.

Number games

Sorting and matching are useful pre-maths skills so get your child involved in sorting out the socks into sizes and pairs. You can introduce your child to shapes by seeing how many square items or round objects she can spot in the room. Get her to count out the plates, knives and forks for dinner. Look at numbers round about you – on houses, on signposts, on packaging. Buy magnetic numbers for the fridge and encourage your child to match them together.

TIDY UP TRICKS

♦ Do not do things for your child because it is easier or more efficient. You are training her for the future.

♦ Accept that your child's standards of tidiness may not be as good as yours. Do not criticise good efforts or redo a job in front of your child.

♦ Give plenty of verbal praise. This could be backed up with a star chart, with a trip out or a present when a certain number of stars have been won. For older children, pocket money could only be given out if the set weekly chores have been done.

♦ Make sure tidying the bedroom is made easy. Do not keep everything on high shelves or in difficult drawers. Labelled stacking crates are useful for toys, as are vegetable racks.

♦ Your child will be more motivated to tidy up if she is proud of her room. Wherever possible, let her choose her curtains, duvet cover or ornaments.

♦ Have very exact aims for each child. This may involve keeping her own room tidy and making her bed. Later, you may give each child specific chores around the house, such as dusting the lounge once a week.

♦ Make it fun, especially for younger children. You could have a game of hotels or hospitals to make the chore more interesting.

♦ Have a race. See if your child can 'beat the clock' when tidying her room, or race brothers and sisters against each other.

♦ Give your child her own cleaning basket. Younger children especially like having their own duster or dustpan and brush.

♦ When your child does not know where something goes, she is most likely just to shove it in the nearest drawer. So have a 'don't know' box in each room and you can help with them at the end of the tidying-up session.

♦ Similarly, each room could have a basket for newly washed and ironed clothes. Each child can then take responsibility for putting them away.

♦ Have a carefully chosen tidy-up time each week for reluctant tidier-uppers. This could be ten or fifteen minutes before a favourite TV programme which should ensure the job gets done quickly and efficiently.

♦ Older children may complain that they have to do more than their younger siblings. Make this fair by giving pocket money based on age.

♦ Have a rota so that everybody takes turns in daily jobs such as laying or clearing the table.

♦ Do not be afraid to use bribes or threats. However, the least stressful way of getting the children to help is to ensure they develop a sense of understanding. Children go through egocentric stages and this may take some time to get through. Hopefully, if you keep explaining *why* you need help with the chores, your children will eventually understand and even *want* to help.

♦ Do not expect too much from pre-school children but once they have settled in at school, gradually introduce more responsibility.

Five minutes at school

♦ Try to speak to your child's teacher at least once a term. If you do not collect your child, you will miss out on the possibility of a grabbed couple of minutes to check that everything is going well. Ask for an appointment, although most schools do have a regular parents' evening.

♦ Do not let guilt lead you into becoming chair-person of the PTA if you just do not have the time. Be realistic about what help and support you can give.

♦ It may be more appropriate for you to donate a raffle prize or a cake rather than give up your one free day to run a bottle stall. Remember that not all parents are working parents.

◆ Ask the school to give you as much warning as possible about activities you will want to attend, such as sports day or the nativity play. Aim for at least one parent to be present and do not feel guilty if it is not you.

◆ If your work place is totally unsympathetic to taking time off for these special events and making it up later, consider giving another excuse. Or just book some of your holiday days well in advance.

◆ The teacher will be aware if you are a working mother and may be reluctant to suggest that you help your child in any specific way at home. If helping your child learn is a high priority, tell the teacher and ask what you can do.

◆ Do get to know your child's friends by inviting them home to play. It may take up some of your time but the chances are your child will get invited back. As your child gets older, it actually entertains her to have a friend and so gives you extra time for something else.

TEENAGERS AND THE FIVE-MINUTE MUM

There are whole books written on the subject of bringing up teenagers as these years bring parenting challenges all of their own. The five-minute mum is likely to have many other commitments by the time the children are teenagers and this is certainly not a bad thing. You will hopefully be setting a good example of how to use time effectively and to the full. You will also, by necessity, be allowing your children to do many more things for themselves and this can only help them in this transition into adulthood. Beware of the following problems you are likely to encounter at this stage.

◆ The teenage years can bring a sudden revival of parental guilt. Teenagers seem to start every other sentence with 'But Paul's mum and dad . . .' Do not let this make you feel guilty. Half of it is not true and anyway, each family must find its own rules and stick to them.

◆ Yes, you will feel like you run a hotel and launderette. Accept that your child is growing away from home and that you will have less time together. However, try to have some meals together during the week even if it means booking it into your diary.

◆ Your teenager should be responsible for her own room. Once she is old enough, she should get her own meals if she is not there at a pre-arranged meal time. Each family must then decide what other duties she will have, whether it's ironing her own clothes or cutting the grass.

◆ You will have to decide what to do if your teenager does not help with the chores. Stopping her from going out is one option. But punishments should not be given without an explanation and discussion. Your teenager should, in principle, agree to share jobs. Make allowances at certain times, such as when exams are on.

◆ Keep rules to a minimum. This would include regular chores to do and coming home at a pre-arranged time. Allow your child as much freedom as you can in other areas such as appearance, decorating her room and choosing friends.

◆ Avoid criticising your child as much as you can and never do it in front of friends. She is likely to be very sensitive at this time.

◆ Avoid shouting matches at all costs. Listen to your child and try to reason with her as calmly as possible.

◆ Allow your child private time on her own. Knock at her door before going in and respect her wish for modesty which tends to come at this stage.

◆ Self-esteem can go down during puberty. Give your child lots of praise and encouragement whenever it is appropriate.

◆ You may find yourself coming in as your child is going out and vice versa. Make an appointment to see your teenager if necessary. This will not be a time for firing endless questions at her but just a time for chatting and being available to listen. But be realistic – your teenager will always have better things to do.

◆ Try not to cling on to those last few months of childhood. Allow your child to develop her independence and individuality.

◆ Try not to get too upset when your child no longer wants to go shopping with you. And when she suddenly walks ten yards behind you in case any of her friends are around, don't take it too personally.

TIME TIPS

◆ Never say 'It's not worth starting anything now . . .' You can do a lot in five minutes. (See Five Minutes Grabbed.)

◆ Doing a job as your child chats to you is not just to your advantage. Surprisingly, many children find it easier to talk out a problem while you are also doing something else.

◆ Hungry teenagers can mean doing extra shops during the week. Buy plenty and hide some fruit and biscuits away for emergencies.

◆ Make at least double the quantity of stew or two pies at a time. Freeze what you do not use and reward yourself with a bake-free week every now and then.

◆ Use the limited time you have at parent–teacher meetings wisely. Do not pour out every detail of all your family problems. The more you say, the less the teacher will say and you will end up uninformed.

◆ Time spent sitting outside your child's school can be used to read, work or relax. Do not use it to get tense or agitated about the fact that your child is always last.

◆ Start to pass on some of your time-management skills to your child.

◆ Have a wash day. If your teenager needs anything washed the day after, she can do it herself.

◆ When your child's bedroom gets so messy you cannot bear to look at it, shut the door.

◆ Once your teenager starts to choose her own clothes, encourage her to keep an eye on labels and look for drip-dry materials rather than dry-clean ones.

FIVE-MINUTE CHECKLIST: ARE YOU LETTING GO?

Time management should be easier with a school-age child who now needs less physical help from you and who can actually help around the house. But, all too often, it just seems to get harder with more washing, more taking and fetching, and more emotional problems to deal with. Take an honest look at how you are managing your child now. Are you allowing her the independence and freedom she needs?

◆ DO YOU ALLOW YOUR CHILD TO HAVE A SAY IN MAJOR FAMILY DECISIONS, SUCH AS WHERE TO GO ON HOLIDAY?

◆ DO YOU ALLOW YOUR CHILD TO HAVE A SAY IN DAY-TO-DAY DECISIONS, SUCH AS WHAT TO HAVE FOR TEA?

◆ DOES YOUR CHILD HAVE AT LEAST PART OF A BEDROOM WALL ON WHICH TO STICK ANYTHING SHE WANTS?

◆ ARE YOU PREPARED TO TAKE YOUR CHILD OUT SHOPPING WITH YOU EVEN WHEN SHE HAS CHOSEN TO LOOK LIKE AN EXTRA FROM 'OLIVER'?

◆ DO YOU HAVE A FEW RULES OF THE HOUSE WHICH YOU APPLY AS CONSISTENTLY AS POSSIBLE?

◆ HAS YOUR CHILD, IN PRINCIPLE, AGREED TO THESE RULES AND IS SHE AWARE OF THEIR PURPOSE?

◆ ARE YOU AWARE THAT WHEN YOUR CHILD FOLDS HER ARMS AND LOOKS AWAY, SHE IS REJECTING WHAT YOU ARE SAYING TO HER?

◆ DOES YOUR CHILD QUESTION SOME OF YOUR DECISIONS?

◆ DOES YOUR CHILD HAVE SOME RESPONSIBILITY FOR HER BEDROOM AND FOR DOING 'HER BIT' TO HELP AROUND THE REST OF THE HOUSE?

◆ DOES YOUR CHILD SHOW SOME UNDERSTANDING OF YOUR NEEDS?

◆ HAVE YOU EVER SAID 'BECAUSE I SAY SO'?

◆ DO YOU BELIEVE A PARENT SHOULD MAKE EVERY SACRIFICE FOR THEIR CHILDREN AND DO AS MUCH AS POSSIBLE FOR THEM?

- ◆ Do you have very set ambitions for your child?

- ◆ Do you decide how your child spends her pocket money?

- ◆ Would your child be quite incapable of getting herself ready for school without any help from you?

- ◆ Do you take complete responsibility for knowing when games/gym/swimming is and making sure the appropriate kit is ready on the right day?

- ◆ Do you make important decisions on behalf of your child?

- ◆ Would your child be unable to get herself a drink/snack/simple meal without your assistance?

- ◆ Have you banned certain friends from your house?

- ◆ Do you always have the last word?

If you answered 'yes' to the first ten questions and 'no' to the rest, you allow your child a lot of freedom and independence. These skills will help with personal development but make sure your child also uses these skills to become a caring and useful member of the family. It may well be a hotel and laundry – but it's not a free one.

Organising Your Time

'Just as something nice and interesting occurs, destiny must intervene with some pressing engagement.'

Conrad Aiken

In order to become an effective parent, especially if you are balancing parenting with other things, you need to be in control of your time. You are not aiming to have more time to do more, but for more time to do less. For time management will involve making choices about how we use our time, discarding all our unnecessary time wasters. It also involves delegating to others. It does not mean cramming as much as we can into our lives. The most useful tools of a good time manager are a pencil and notebook. By writing down what you do and crossing off what you need not do, by making lists of priorities and crossing them off as achievements, and by having written reminders around you, you can suddenly feel in control.

We all have the same amount of time available but like furnishing the same room, we will all distribute it differently. What does not work is just muddling through trying to do as much as you can and then gradually feeling that you just cannot cope. What also does not work is clinging on to past habits when your life changes with the addition of children or the beginning of a new job (or both). You may no longer have time to iron the sheets or bake your own bread but no one will suffer if these activities are dropped.

You need to be in control of your own time in order to delegate time to yourself, otherwise your own needs can often be left at the bottom of the pile and never considered. You need to be in control of your time to change your daily panic into a relaxed approach to your life, however busy. You need to be in control of your time to ensure that one part of your life does not take up more time than the parts (such as parenting) which are most important to you.

SETTING GOALS

You will need long-term goals and short-term goals. You probably already have some idea of your long-term goals although it does help to write them down and put them in order of priority. Once you know what your long-term goals are, it makes the short-term or daily goals easier to make. For example, a long-term goal may be to raise independent children who are nevertheless close to you. In the short-term, this will mean allocating time to be with your children but having a lifestyle which enables them to learn self-help skills and skills of independence – this may involve going to a nursery each day. Similarly, you may have a long-term goal involving advancement in your career and your short-term goals will enable you to work towards this gradually.

If long-term goals prove difficult to make, imagine yourself as a ninety-year-old looking back over your life. What do you want to say you have achieved? Now write your own tombstone or obituary. What do you want on it, 'She kept the house looking nice' or 'She was a successful author and mother of two delightful children'? Once you have set your goals down, you may need to make some changes in your life. These could be quite drastic, such as turning down a promotion to enable you to spend more time with your children, or taking on a nanny to enable you to do further training.

Always consider any long-term planning when you are feeling well, relaxed and positive. Do not let a temporary mood or tiredness affect such important decisions. Goals should be achievable but realistic and once you have set your goals you need to break them up into small stages and tackle one small step at a time. This keeps you moving toward achieving your goals and gives you the feeling of success.

Long-term goals   Do not set strong limits to what you might achieve in the long term. You need to be realistic but aim for high achievement. Review your long-term goals every six months.

Short-term goals   Slice long-term goals into achievable components and you have your short-term goals. When setting a goal, ask 'What?', 'Why?', 'When?' and 'How?' 'How' is often the missing item. Be specific when deciding *how* your goal will be achieved. Set time limits, avoiding the 'I'll do it when . . .' scenario (e.g. 'I'll do it when the children are older', 'I'll do it when I've finished this diet.') This way of thinking can also involve rushing children on to the next stage.

MAKING PRIORITIES

You will want to make some goals into long-term priorities, and this will affect how you manage your time now. You will also need daily priorities. To sit down and make these priorities will clearly take up time in itself, but it is well spent for it will save time later and help you feel in control. To start with, you need to know exactly how you are spending your time now. When you are just 'muddling along', you can have quite the wrong idea of exactly how your time is divided up. Guilt can make you feel you are barely spending five minutes a day with your children when in truth you are spending at least three hours. Time wasting (sometimes just wasted in the process of worrying) can eat into either work or family time. So, to start with, walk around with a clock and time your activities for a week. Put these into major categories – perhaps parenting, work, travel, household chores and relaxation. Draw a large circle and divide it up into segments representing these main activities. Make the segments an appropriate size according to the percentage of time spent on each activity. Now write down what percentage of time you would like to spend on each major activity. If you would like to spend more time with your children or less time travelling, then you need to work out how you can change the relative sizes of the segments. Remember that time is finite so if you want more time for yourself or your partner for example, you will need to spend less time on something else. Aim to change the size of the segments to meet your own priorities. You may feel that you could not possibly cut down the size of any of the segments and this is where your short-term planning of priorities can help.

Again, look at what you are doing currently to start with. Write down, in more detail this time, how you spend your time each day. When you look at your list, highlight any activities that could have been delegated and those which need not have been done at all. Look at the remaining items and see which took you longer than they should and which had to be rushed. Now add to the list anything which you would have liked to have spent time on that day but were unable to. With this in mind, make your list of priorities for the next day and week. Only put essential items on the daily plan, the rest can go on the weekly list. Put them in order of priority, cross off any which really do not need doing, or else transfer them to a long-term list. Delegate anything you can and you will immediately feel more in control.

TACKLING PRIORITY TASKS

Some people like to deal with the most difficult or least favourite activity first, tackling procrastination head on. Other people prefer to tackle the shorter or easier tasks, ticking them off as they go along to give a sense of achievement.

For activities which you tend to avoid at all costs (ironing perhaps), try a different approach. Try doing five- or ten-minute timed stints, with breaks in between to do more enjoyable tasks.

Re-prioritise activities which are not completed, either to the next day's/week's list or to a long-term list.

Put time estimates on your schedule. If the activity takes you a lot longer, work out why. If it was because of interruptions, see how these could have been avoided. Or perhaps you have more productive times of the day because of your routine or because of yourself. In this case, tackle difficult tasks at your productive times and easier, quicker tasks at other times.

Do not be a perfectionist. For parents returning to work, this may mean changing standards a little. Always ask yourself 'Does it matter if . . .' such as 'Does it matter if my children have fish and chips tonight?' or 'Does it matter if I have not dusted the lounge?'

Be flexible. You do not always want your home life run like a business even though you feel it helps. Occasionally you can be impulsive or improvise.

If you are unable to tackle all the activities on your list, you may have too much on your schedule. Trying to do too much in too little time equals stress. Look at your list again and be brash – cut out anything you can.

You may have to allocate a set amount of time to a task and then stop at the end of that time. This particularly applies to housework which tends to expand to fit the time available.

Reward yourself. So often we only give time to ourselves when we have satisfied the needs of other people. Time for yourself should be a weekly or even daily priority. It can help to tackle less-satisfying tasks if you are then going to reward yourself, with anything from a hot bath to a favourite drink.

If you have difficulty getting started, get back to your paper and pencil. Write down all the reasons for not tackling a task and all the reasons you should. The reasons for getting started should look much stronger for priority tasks.

SETTING LIMITS

There is a limit to the number of hours in the day and there is a limit to your mental and physical energy. Any goals you set have therefore got to be realistic and achievable. You may need to cut things out or cut corners. Set realistic limits to the following:

◆ The number of hours you work.
◆ The amount of unpaid overtime you do.
◆ The number of chores you can do in a week.
◆ The amount of support you give to your children's school or

nursery. You may be able to make or buy a cake but you will not be able to work on the cake stall all day Saturday.

◆ The number of clubs or events you transport your children to.You will need a minimum amount of time to be spent on yourself or by yourself.

THE DAILY ROUTINE

Some of your time will already be allocated. For example, you may have to leave for work at a set time, or be on the bus for a certain amount of time. Your child, consequently, may have to be at nursery for some hours and once you have confidence in his care, that time is already allocated without any input from you. Write down the flexible times of the day when you can allocate activities according to the needs of yourself and the whole family.

Firstly, make sure your pre-allocated time remains in its time slot. If you are always doing extra time at work ask yourself why. If there is some unwritten law that you work longer than your allocated hours, you may want to question this. If you are in a very high paid job and happy to do the hours that it takes, fine. If not, be assertive and stick to the hours you are paid to do, within reason. It could be that you are working longer hours because you are just not working very efficiently. In this case, you will need to apply time-management techniques at work. This will include delegating, making use of efficient times of the day and prioritising.

Some of the time left may need to be fairly structured. Morning time in a house of two working parents is a typical example. There will be no spare time to be flexible, you will simply have an aim of getting everybody to their allocated places on time. This flows most smoothly if some preparation is done the night before to avoid last minute searches for lunch boxes and the like. You should also be prepared for all disasters – this may involve wearing overalls over your work clothes until the last minute to keep baby's sticky fingers at bay.

At the end of the day, you can probably be more flexible with the time. Apart from preparing food (which can, of course, be delegated) you may have some realistic aims of 'jobs' to be done. Spending time with your children is likely to be a high priority but do not forget to have some time to yourself now and again.

TIME SAVERS

- ◆ A noticeboard in the kitchen with urgent numbers on and all your reminders to yourself or your partner. Trying to remember everything takes up energy and causes stress.
- ◆ Be prepared. Get clothes out the night before. Know exactly what you will do if your child is ill or the car will not start.
- ◆ Do one big shop a week and delegate this occasionally, if possible. Have a list of what to buy tied in with the weekly menus and if you run out of someone's favourite biscuits halfway through the week, then they have to make do until the next shop.
- ◆ Have a basket at the top and bottom of the stairs. Put things in that need to be moved up or down to save unnecessary running around.
- ◆ Have a lost property cupboard and encourage the children to look there for missing items. They will gradually take more responsibility for their own belongings.
- ◆ Take something with you to do if ever you are likely to be held up at appointments or at the train station. Feeling that you are wasting valuable time can leave you feeling very stressed.
- ◆ Stick to your list.
- ◆ Other people are potentially your biggest time savers. Delegate completely so that the other person has full responsibility.
- ◆ Be assertive. Practise saying no, practise disagreeing with someone and practise delegating. You can do this by acting out situations with a group of friends. You can end up doing low priority tasks because you just cannot say no. You can end up doing it yourself because you do not like to ask.
- ◆ Use tidy-up short cuts. A bunch of flowers on the table can

make the whole room look different. Just do what is necessary and remember that the houses of non-working parents often look more untidy – after all, there are people there all day.

♦ Not giving up what you really enjoy, but making it easier for yourself. For example, if you like entertaining, have a barbecue or pot-luck supper instead of a four-course gourmet meal.

TIME WASTERS

♦ No self-imposed deadlines, no priority schedule, insufficient delegation, the inability to say no, confused objectives.

♦ Perfectionism. Paying too much attention to minor details.

♦ Being resistant to change. When your lifestyle changes or when your children get older, this will instigate changes in other areas of your life.

♦ Trying to do too much in too little time – this can result in you doing very little in an awful lot of time.

♦ Interruptions when you least need them. Sometimes you need to arrange a time when you can shut your door and get on with it.

♦ Confusion. Although you may need to cut corners as far as housework is concerned, you do need some level of tidiness in order to know where everything is. Know where to lay your hands on anything you might need at a moment's notice but do not worry if it has a layer of dust on it.

♦ Worrying. Worrying, especially about what might happen, takes up a lot of mental energy and is unproductive. Talking things over with your partner or a friend is likely to be more productive than solitary worrying.

♦ Telephone calls. If you allocate some time to help your child with homework or just to watch his favourite programme together, the telephone is bound to ring. Ignore it or get an answerphone. It is bound to be an old friend who you have not spoken to for years and will consequently take up the next hour of your allocated time. An answerphone means that you can phone back when the children are in bed.

◆ Self-imposed interruptions. If the post arrives, we tend to stop what we are doing to read it. If the newspaper comes, we just stop what we are doing to check the weather forecast. Some interruptions are self imposed. So take note of when you do it, leave a written reminder to yourself in a prominent place and then give up this time-wasting habit. It often takes longer to complete tasks if we have to pick up something again in the middle.

◆ Too much haste. This does not just refer to what you do but to making decisions, planning and preparation. Time can be wasted by not putting time aside to plan your day and to ensure that you make appropriate decisions.

◆ Being unfit and tired. It may seem like you are wasting time by going to bed early and setting aside time for exercise. But this will save you time in the long run, as will ensuring you stop for healthy meals. You will also be revived after a break, and many working parents like to keep their lunch-break as precisely that – a break. A dash round the supermarket is hardly a break.

◆ Labour intensive purchases. Never buy dry clean clothes, food which involves long and intensive preparation (unless this type of cooking is a form of relaxation for you) or games for your children which need half an hour to assemble every time you use them.

TIME AND MONEY

Money can buy time. Some people will need to consider their budget quite carefully to decide how much money they can allocate to time-saving devices. Extra child care or help in the house and garden could mean an opportunity to work more hours, so you will need to weigh up all the choices.

Labour-saving devices include a tumble-drier, freezer, microwave, dishwasher, domestic help, gardener, slow cooker, duvets and self-cleaning cooker. The most useful of these is a deep-freeze but use it to the full. It can enable you to do a big monthly shop with small weekly shops in between. You may even want to have a cooking afternoon to prepare the meals for the whole week. With a freezer you can always have food available, even when you do not have time to do your weekly shop. Also, you can easily buy food which any member of the family over the age of 10 can prepare.

Labour intensive devices include clothes which have to be dry-cleaned, pets, varnished nails and a hairstyle which requires a great deal of attention every morning. Choose brands very carefully – some kitchen equipment may take ages to clean after use, for example.

If you decide to employ someone to help in the house, try to have a thorough clean and tidy-up first so that she or he knows the standard to work towards. Sack incompetent cleaners immediately and do not employ a cleaner who intends to bring children with her. You may find it just as economical to employ a cleaning firm to have a blitz on the house once a month.

TIME OFF

As well as allocating time for relaxation during the week, you will want to make the most of weekends and holidays. Get right away for your holidays whenever you can. If you do stay at home, go out on picnics and walks and limit the time you spend on household chores. Try to have one of the weekend days set aside entirely for relaxation together. Unwinding will make you more efficient during the week and spending a long period of time in the company of your children will be beneficial to the whole family.

WHAT WE LEARN FROM BUSINESS

Business courses give us two useful acronyms which can be applied to parenting time management. The first is SMART – specific, manageable, achievable, realistic and time targeted. This is a useful description of what a goal should be. The other acronym is SWOT – strengths, weaknesses, opportunities, threats. This is useful when making decisions about how to use or allocate your time. Simply write down these four aspects of anything you are considering doing but are not sure of. Another technique is the journal technique where you write down all your thoughts about the proposed decision as they come into your head. When you have finished, divide them all into pros and cons and note which thoughts came first and are therefore likely to carry more weight.

Time management in business is applicable to parenting. Even in the office, you need to arrange uninterrupted time each day, you need to delegate, write lists, have goals and be assertive. With parenting, you are trying to manage the rest of your time so efficiently that you have time to enjoy the parenting side of your life thoroughly. Some aspects of parenting may seem like hard work, whether they be potty training or helping with maths homework. But mostly parenting is exceptionally rewarding and enjoyable. If you can switch off the other pressures of life and relax, parenting can be the best part of the day and of your life. If being a parent and spending time with the children is your ultimate goal and priority, everything else should fall into place and get into perspective. Young children have a habit of reminding us just how trivial that work worry is.

20 WAYS TO WASTE YOUR TIME

♦ Sitting on the bus or train. You can use this time for something else – relaxation. Worrying about the day ahead does not achieve anything.

♦ Worrying about the amount of work you have to do. Break it down into smaller goals and get on with it. Worrying takes time and energy.

♦ Choosing what to wear. Get out what you need the night before and stick to it.

♦ Ironing bedding, night wear, handkerchiefs or underwear.

♦ Tidying up after the children when they should have done it themselves.

- Cleaning the lounge because it is your day to do it. If it looks all right, leave it and do something with a higher priority.
- Cutting the crusts off the sandwiches.
- Talking to a friend on the phone for half an hour when you are seeing her tomorrow night.
- Cleaning and polishing the car every Sunday.
- Drying the dishes.
- Hand-washing clothes.
- Looking for an essential list, memo or letter which could have been pinned to a noticeboard.
- Going to the shop to buy the marmalade you forgot. Have jam until shopping day.
- Cooking separate meals for a child who is fussy about food. If he does not like what is in front of him, give him bread, cheese and an apple.
- Waiting for appointments. Phone first and ask if they are running late. Or take something with you to do.
- Searching the shops for something specific. Phone round first to find out who stocks it.
- Searching for older children. Children who are old enough to go and call on friends can cause you to search or phone for them. Get them to call you or report back at regular intervals instead.
- Shoving everything into a cupboard, under the cushions or behind the couch haphazardly. Have a place for everything and, if necessary, a temporary hold area. This saves time doing a massive sort-out later or trying to locate missing items.
- Peeling fruit or vegetables that do not need peeling.
- Washing-up your coffee cup. Put things in to soak until you have enough to make washing-up worthwhile.

WHAT ARE YOUR MOST VALUED TIME TIPS?

Parents answered . . .

'Shopping by mail order – I always used to be rather snooty about this but now I swear by it.'

Karen Patterson

'The Chinese take-away is my most treasured labour-saving device – when I'm running late, I can suddenly catch up on all the time lost and gain time too.'

Melanie Brown

'We have one corner of the lounge which is always neat and tidy and where we can relax at the end of the day. I think by nature we're both tidiness freaks but with us both working we have had to compromise.'

Ken Stock

'Going out for Christmas dinner. We've done it ever since I went back to work and it's worth every penny.'

Carol Bates

'Get to bed as early as possible to build up your strength for the next day.'

Carol Dronside

'Think of work and home commitments as being very separate. That way you feel that in each place, you are having a rest from the other.'

Kathy Sherrit

'Do all the things which are important and leave the unimportant ones until they become unimportant or unnecessary.'

Jenny Heath

FIVE-MINUTE CHECKLIST: ARE YOU IN CONTROL OF YOUR TIME?

◆ DO YOU EVER GET STUCK ON THE PHONE WITH SOMEONE YOU WOULD RATHER SPEAK TO LATER?

◆ IS YOUR PIN BOARD LITTERED WITH OUT OF DATE INFORMATION?

◆ DO YOU HAVE AT LEAST ONE KITCHEN DRAWER WHERE EVERYTHING GETS SHOVED WHEN YOU DO NOT KNOW WHERE TO PUT IT?

◆ DO YOU FEEL EMBARRASSED WHEN A GUEST COMES INTO YOUR LESS THAN PERFECT HOUSE?

◆ DOES EVERYONE SEEM TO SHOUT AT EACH OTHER IN THE MORNINGS AS YOU ALL STRUGGLE TO GET OFF ON TIME?

◆ DO YOUR CHILDREN RELY ON YOU TO KNOW WHICH DAY IS FOOTBALL, BROWNIES OR A SCHOOL TRIP?

◆ DO YOU USE TIME OFF WORK TO GIVE YOU A CHANCE TO CATCH UP WITH DOMESTIC DUTIES?

◆ CAN YOU MANAGE WITHOUT A LIST?

◆ DO YOU LEAVE RELAXATION UNTIL EVERYTHING ELSE IS DONE?

◆ DO YOU TAKE ONE DAY AT A TIME?

◆ GIVE YOURSELF A POINT FOR EVERY QUESTION YOU CAN HONESTLY ANSWER 'NO' TO.

It is very unlikely that you will have been able to answer 'no' to all these. There are bound to be areas of your life which need change, so tackle one thing at a time and gradually gain control. Give yourself six months and then try the checklist again.

CHAPTER EIGHT

How Not to be a Guilty Parent

'As innocent as a child ... as guilty as a working mother in a traffic jam.'

Sara Welch

Nearly all parents feel guilty from time to time, whether or not they go out to work. This seems to come from a desire to be a perfect parent and never quite reaching those very high and often unrealistic ideals we all set for ourselves. Working parents often have added guilt, feeling they should be with their children and not at work at all. This becomes highlighted when a child is taken ill at nursery or performs in a school concert. The 'I should have been there' syndrome hits all working parents at least once during the early years. However, it should not be forgotten that even a parent who is at home 24 hours a day is susceptible to parental guilt. Sometimes, we *know* the guilt is unjustified and even downright silly, yet the feelings can still be very strong and emotionally charged. It is essential to acknowledge our feelings of guilt and deal with them effectively. Otherwise, guilty feelings can lead us to act irrationally, spoil our children and leave us feeling emotionally drained. Guilt feelings take up time and energy and stop us feeling in control of our lives. Firstly, it is important to know that we are not alone. Secondly, we need to confront our feelings and then eliminate any unfounded guilt. It is all too easy for parents to focus on the times when family life does not run entirely smoothly and to forget that everyone is basically happy and well-adjusted. Parents can spend hours worrying about a minor hiccup and forget about the main issue, which is that children have a stable and loving environment.

REASONS ALL PARENTS CAN FEEL GUILTY

Not spending enough time together

Working parents may be especially susceptible to this but it can hit all parents. We cannot spend all our time with the children and neither should we. Children need time to themselves and time to relate to other children and adults. When we actually sit down and work out how much time we spend with the children, it is always more than we think. Time spent dressing, feeding and washing your child has value too – you do not have to be reading stories for it to be enjoyable and worthwhile. You must have time for yourself and time for your partner if you are to maintain a balance in your life. Your children will benefit from a refreshed parent rather than a tired, stale one who has just spent the last 24 hours in their company.

Being bad-tempered with your child

If you are *always* bad-tempered with your child, then perhaps you do need to look at why this is happening. It may just be a symptom of tiredness or stress, in which case you need to delegate some of your responsibilities to someone else. Or else you need to gain control of your life with the time-management techniques outlined in Chapter 7. However, it is more likely that you are just bad-tempered occasionally. This may be justified – after all, children are no more perfect than parents are. Your bad temper may let your child know that what she is doing is unacceptable which means your mood is not entirely fruitless. As your child matures, it is a good idea to explain to her *why* you feel in a bad mood. Even very young children can understand that you are tired and have been working hard. Children need to learn that you are only human and that they should be considerate towards you. Only feel guilty if bad temper gets out of hand, then look to change the reasons behind it.

Not providing your child with everything

Limits to the family budget may mean that your child does not have everything she wants. This is different from everything she needs. She needs food, shelter and love, which you provide. Giving your child everything she wants is spoiling her, which is very harmful. Your child will learn that there are limits to the family budget and that there will always be people with more than her. This is a lesson we all have to learn, and the sooner the better. Whatever your financial circumstances, you need to make priorities. Once your child is old enough to appreciate money, give pocket money so that she, too, can prioritise. Make sure you know why you want to buy your child more – it could be out of guilt. It is far better to sort out those feelings before guilt buying takes over.

Treating your children unequally

You may find you are giving more time to one of your children. Do not feel guilty about this as it is often entirely necessary. Children of different ages have different needs or one child may be going through a 'difficult patch'. Remember, your children are not timing you and will barely notice if one is getting a little more of your time for a while. Try to spend a little time on your own with each child if you can.

Wanting time to yourself

We all need time to ourselves. It makes us better parents and allows our children to spend time on their own or with your partner or other adult. Yet, many parents feel guilty when they are not with the children. This is unrealistic and unfounded.

Not always putting your children first

Of course, your children's needs will have a very high priority but it is not always possible to put them first nor should you for your own, as well as their, sake.

REASONS WORKING PARENTS FEEL ESPECIALLY GUILTY

Leaving your child with someone else when she is better off with you

She is not necessarily better off being with you all the time, even if you are the most important adult in her life. Focus on the advantages to your child in sharing her care. There are so many, you will soon realise how unfounded your guilt is. Studies have shown that children who have good quality nursery care concentrate better at school and have better communication and social skills. Your child will be more adaptable and be able to form relationships with other adults and children more readily. She will also gain, indirectly, from the fact that you work. Not only financially, but by having quality time with a parent who appreciates every minute spent with her children.

The carer seems to spend more time with your child than you

Remember that time together is special to you both and that you have a special type of relationship with your child. Studies show that even children bought up in an Israeli kibbutz, where child care is done communally by designated people, make their closest relationships with their parents.

Not spending enough time together as a whole family

A busy lifestyle may mean that it is either you or your partner looking after the children and that times all together are rare. Your children will not suffer from this arrangement although it is worth making an effort to have some time as a complete family for the enjoyment of you all.

Not going on enough outings

Children do not always want special trips out, especially if they have been at a nursery most of the week. They prefer time with you rather than specific outings, although a trip out may mean that your time together is not interrupted. Do not make your weekends action-packed to compensate for the limited time you spend together during the week. Parents at home with the children all day are unlikely to be going out on special trips all week so your child is not missing out in any way.

Missing out on your child's development

If your child should take her first steps or say her first words while you are not there, you have every reason to feel disappointed. This can spark off guilt feelings although your child will not be thinking that you should have been watching. Whatever she did, she will do it again for you later and the pleasure and enjoyment can still be as good.

Your child has to cope with early independence

This is not necessarily a negative thing. The ultimate aim of rearing children is to teach them to be gradually more independent so that they can cope without you. Your children may seem to be growing up too quickly but can only gain by having good independent skills which will help them through the school years.

Guilt induced by other people

Some people may have very set views about families with two working parents. These views may remain inflexible and unchanged even when your child displays every sign of happiness. Ignore any unwanted advice and views of others – only you know whether your arrangements are working out well for you and your children. This unwanted advice is usually littered with guilt-inducing phrases such as 'latch-key kids' or 'absent parents'. Laugh about it, if you can!

Cobweb guilt

Do not feel guilty if your house is not as clean or tidy as it used to be. Your children will not even notice, let alone mind.

GUILT BEHAVIOUR

The problem with guilt is not so much the emotional strain it can put on us as the things it makes us do. If you recognise any of these symptoms of guilt, you know it needs tackling before it gets even more out of hand.

Guilt buying

Do not be tempted to compensate for being away at work by buying everything your child wants. By all means give her the occasional treat, but spoiling her with extra material goods will not do her any good. Before long, your child will learn that she can get anything by inducing guilt feelings in you. Compensate by giving your child extra time at the weekend rather than more toys. Children who get everything gain no satisfaction from the things they have and they start to focus on the things they have not got and think they need. A child with a lot of toys is not necessarily spoilt but a child who gets everything she asks for probably is – it is how and why she gets them that counts.

Spoiling

Guilt buying may be part of spoiling but this also includes letting your child 'get away with' anything. The last thing you want to do when you have been at work all day is to reprimand your child for bad behaviour. If you feel bad about being away from her, you can mistakenly think that she will not like you if you tell her off as well. You already think you are a bad parent and do not want to make it worse. All children need structured guidelines for behaviour and will become confused if you are inconsistent in your approach. It is too much for a child to decide the limits of her behaviour – she needs this decided for her even if she does test it out occasionally. A spoilt child becomes selfish, cannot share and does not take the feelings of others into account, seeing herself as the most important person. Beware of apologising straight after reprimanding her for unacceptable behaviour unless you have genuinely over-reacted.

Being demanding

Your child may certainly demand more of you and you will do your best to accommodate those demands. However, parents too can be over-demanding of their child. It can be disappointing to get home from work only to find your child wrapped up in some private game. Or to plan an outing one Saturday only to find she wants to play out with friends. Take this complete lack of 'clingyness' as a sign that your child is happy and settled. Do not be tempted to force your child into your company – she will soon finish her game and want your attention. Just ensure that your child knows you are there to listen when she needs you.

Thinking your work is the cause of all problems

Children will sometimes have tantrums, be naughty, demanding or even downright irritating. This may be because of their age – what child has not gone through the terrible two stage – or because they are testing out the rules, or simply because they are tired. No child behaves perfectly all the time and we should not blame every slight misdemeanour on the fact that we work. Do families who have one parent at home have better behaved children? Of course not. Similarly, it is easy to blame problems at work on the fact that we also have children to care for.

Action-packed evenings and weekends

Ask yourself why you are taking your three-year-old to every park within a twenty-park radius. Why is your four-year-old being dragged around every museum in the county? And why does she attend five different clubs a week, filling in any spare moments by looking at flashcards with you? If this is really what you and your child want, fine. But make sure that it is not guilt making you fill in every second with a structured activity. Children need some time to themselves and so do you. You also need time relaxing together. Involve your child in choosing what you do with your spare time and make sure you are not both exhausted by Monday morning.

Chopping and changing child care

If you are constantly changing your child care in search of the perfect arrangement, do question your motives. This is often another symptom of guilt.

GUILT BASHERS

Talk about it

You are not alone with your feelings and when you talk about them with other parents, you will start to see how ridiculous they often are. Laugh and joke about them and get an outsider to help get your feelings into perspective.

Be positive

Feeling guilty is not all bad. It means that you want to be a good parent and that you care about your family. Sometimes, guilt can be a warning that something is wrong. If, for example, you feel guilty about leaving your child with a child minder, examine your feelings to see if you are being ridiculous or if, in fact, the child minder is not satisfactory.

Look at your child

If your child is happy, contented and settled then the chances are that you have nothing whatsoever to feel guilty about. If, however, your child is unsettled and you feel guilty, take a look and see if any changes need to be made. You may need a change of carer or a change in your approach. Giving up work completely is unlikely to be the change you need. Tune into your child's needs and you will soon achieve a good balance.

Listen to your child

When you talk to your child about your work, you will find that she is proud of what you do. You can also ask older children specific questions which prove what she is gaining in thoughts and attitudes. One psychologist asked children how a man in the moon would view men and women on earth. Children with two working parents described people with less sexual stereotyping. Ask your child this question and then ask her what she wants to do when she grows up. Children with two working parents are often quite ambitious from an early age to get an interesting job. They tend to view work in a very positive way.

Get your emotions in balance

Write down what you feel a parent should or should not feel guilty about and then look at your list in relation to your own feelings. Make sure you are not worrying or feeling guilty about something that might happen. If, underneath, you feel that working is somehow wrong, you are more likely to find problems that do not exist. Talk to other working parents and talk to their children too. Older children with working parents may illustrate the confidence and independence which you want for your child.

Take account of your physical state

You are tired, overworked and stressed. In this situation, you are bound to find problems to feel guilty about even if none exist. Have an early night or treat yourself to a massage. Then tackle any problems that are left.

Look on the bright side

Rather than reprimanding yourself for being late for the nativity play, congratulate yourself for getting there in time for your child's entrance. Rather than feeling guilty because there was no one to take your child to Angela's party, make a date to take Angela on a special picnic with you.

Focus on the benefits

There are many benefits to you and your child when both parents work. Focus on these rather than any possible negative effects. Negative effects only occur when your child care is not good enough and this can be changed. Make a list of what you all gain. This will include job satisfaction, maintaining a balanced life, financial benefits, your child's improved social skills, confidence, skills of independence and communication abilities. Your child will also have good role models who are not sexual stereotypes. She will learn that women can work and men can cook. There will be other benefits which are particular to your family and your circumstances. Write them down and pin them on the wall.

Talk to housewives

You will be surprised when you talk to a parent who is home all day to find that her children are not constantly out on trips, painting and learning to read. These children do not seem to have great advantages over yours and the parent at home has other commitments too. Even thinking back to your own childhood can help, if you had a parent at home all day. Do you remember a mother who was constantly available?

'DO YOU EVER FEEL GUILTY?'

Parents answered . . .

'Getting phone calls and having to attend to work problems whilst I am playing with Anna.'

John Robertson

Solution: Get an answerphone. You can always leave a message saying you are there and will get back to the caller as soon as you can take a break.

'During my time off, I have to do chores, such as shopping, which Steven does not enjoy.'

Heather Smith

Solution: Why does he not enjoy shopping? It may be because you are tense or rushed. Try getting your partner to help or make it an outing by rewarding you both with a drink in the café or a mini-picnic afterwards.

'I lost a good job because of poor child care facilities and wished the children had never been born. Not out loud but I still felt so terribly guilty immediately afterwards. It was like a physical blow. I still feel guilty about it now even though I can rationalise it – it was just down to the strain.'

Anon.

Solution: The writer already knows she should not still feel guilty about something that she only thought years ago. Always focus on the children, who cannot be affected by a bad thought which was only temporary anyway. It does help to talk these feelings out. You would find that most parents will have had similar feelings at similar times of stress.

'I work two days a week further away and sometimes stay over. I have been known to bring home toys if I have been away those two days.'

Sybil Clews

Solution: No real problem here. Buying something when you go away is not a bad thing so long as your child does not greet you with her hand held out – then you know it has got out of hand. The best sort of treat is when your child leasts expects it and not when she has been nagging you for it. If you acknowledge that you are in danger of guilt buying then you will keep it under control.

'There is immense pressure put on working mothers by the non-working mothers' lobby. I went back to work in the face of adversity.'

Diana Smith

Solution: This works both ways. Some working parents are quite critical of those who stay at home. Ignore criticism from those who do not know your circumstances. Focus on your child. If she is settled and happy about your particular arrangement then all is well.

'I feel guilty that I do not put in the additional hours at work that other people do.'

Lynne Macleod

Solution: Good time management should enable you to do your job well in the hours available. It is better to be efficient than busy. If your family is now a high priority and you are doing your job efficiently then there is nothing to feel guilty about.

'I feel guilty if I send them to school a bit off-colour with the proviso that if they get worse, school will let me know.'

Winnie Taylor

Solution: No problem here. The school certainly would let you know if your child was ill. Make sure the school know where you are at all times. While you would want to keep a really sick child at home, letting your child cope with minor sniffles will set a good trend for the future. You would not stop every time you sneezed, but some people do.

'I feel guilty if I am late to collect him.'

Andrea Logan

Solution: You should only feel guilty if this is a regular occurrence, in which case you would clearly need to change your schedule in some way.

FIVE-MINUTE CHECKLIST:
HAS GUILT GOT OUT OF HAND?

◆ ARE YOU PREPARED TO IGNORE YOUR CHILD'S SCREAMS FOR YET MORE SWEETS WHEN YOU ARE OUT?

◆ IS A TANTRUM BEST DEALT WITH BY GIVING YOUR CHILD A BIG CUDDLE AND A LOT OF UNDERSTANDING?

◆ ARE YOU HAPPY TO BUY YOUR CHILD AN OCCASIONAL TREAT WHEN SHE HAS BEEN GOOD ON A SHOPPING TRIP?

◆ DO YOU LIKE TO SPEND FRIDAY NIGHT PLANNING EVERY MOMENT OF YOUR WEEKEND?

◆ DO YOU TRY TO IGNORE BAD BEHAVIOUR FROM YOUR CHILD WHEN YOU RETURN FROM WORK?

◆ DO YOU FEEL TIME SPENT DOING YOUR FAVOURITE HOBBY IS A BIT OF AN INDULGENCE?

◆ ARE YOU THRILLED WHEN YOUR CHILD'S CARER TELLS YOU OF YOUR CHILD'S LATEST BIG ACHIEVEMENT?

◆ DO YOU KEEP YOUR CHILD UP VERY LATE TO MAKE UP FOR LOST TIME?

◆ CAN YOU RELAX AND ENJOY PLAYING WITH YOUR CHILD WHEN YOU CAN WRITE YOUR NAME ON A DUSTY TABLE?

◆ DOES YOUR CHILD HAVE MORE THAN FIVE TOYS WHICH SHE WANTED DESPERATELY BUT HAS HARDLY EVER PLAYED WITH?

If you answered 'yes' to the first and then to every other question (and 'no' to the rest), any guilt feelings you may have had are well in control.

CHAPTER NINE

Making the Most of Your Partner

*'Modern drugs are wonderful. They enable a wife with
pneumonia to nurse her husband through 'flu.'*

Faith Hines and Pam Brown

Typically, women do more of the housework and parenting and
men work longer hours and earn more. However, everyone's situation is different and, in each partnership, parents need to sort out
their own roles and responsibilities according to their individual
circumstances. There are some traps you can fall into. Firstly, why,
if you both do full-time jobs, is the male partner somehow
expected to put more hours in at work? Should this be challenged
with his employer? Secondly, why if you both work full time does
the responsibility of the children and home invariably fall on the
mother, even if the chores are divided equally? After all, the
responsibility and delegation take up time and energy too.
Thirdly, why do partners often disagree about the exact amount
the father does? Typically, fathers feel they do their share while
their partners know that they do not. It may also be that one
parent seems to get all the good jobs while the other does the
rotten ones. However, you will need to be realistic. If one partner
has less responsibility outside the home, it would clearly work
best if that partner takes on more responsibility in the home and
with the family. And if the parents are separated, both will want
and need to take on some of the responsibility and care of the
children.

The secret of a good partnership is that both sides feel happy
with the arrangements for sharing jobs and responsibilities. Too

often, there is no formal division of labour. Both partners just muddle along doing what they have always done even when there has been a change of circumstances such as a new baby or one partner returning to work. This non-arrangement often leads one partner to feel hard-done-by, resentful and frustrated. This partner may then start to nag which is a symptom of this frustration. Far better to sit down and make some sensible decisions about how you are going to run the home and family; decisions which suit everyone.

THE ART OF DELEGATION

In most cases, women take on the main responsibility of the home and family. It is therefore the usual case that they are doing the delegating to their partners. Firstly, the very idea of sharing the responsibilities needs to be discussed. After all, women will already have given considerable thought to how child care and work will fit together and how having children will affect their job prospects and income. Men, on the other hand, may have given it no thought at all.

How much and what you delegate will depend on your circumstances but you will get the most out of your partner if you start by delegating the things he feels most comfortable and confident with. Do not just delegate the 'chore' but delegate the responsibility for that chore as well. Delegation is of little use if you have to check that it has been done. Once you have delegated, let go and accept how your partner tackles a job. It may be true that you would do it differently or even better but if you truly let go, you will accept your partner's way of doing things. Remember, once all the tasks have been shared between you then there is no permanent state of delegating, just shared care and responsibilities. You will not be re-delegating regular tasks all the time. However, there may be times when you will be delegating more to your partner, or vice versa, as a temporary arrangement, perhaps because you have taken on an extra challenge at work or because you are unwell. It is important to have a totally flexible arrangement even though you have sorted out the main responsibilities between you.

If you still feel that the balance is uneven, make a list of what you do and what your partner does. Does it seem a reasonable division in relation to your other commitments? If not, look at your list again and mark what else you could delegate. Show your partner the list so that he agrees it is a fair division. Talk about who does what when you both have time for a relaxed, effective chat. Do not leave it until resentment builds up and it is at risk of becoming a shouting match.

WHY MAKE THE MOST OF YOUR PARTNER?

Making the most of your partner is clearly going to help with the management of your own time. However, sharing responsibilities is also going to be of benefit to both your partner and your children.

Advantages to your partner

◆ The more child care he does, the better his opportunity of building up a good relationship with his children.
◆ He will be well equipped to step in with total child care in cases of emergency (a sick child or you going away on business).
◆ Participating in the practicalities of family life will create a better balance in your partner's life.
◆ The caring side of your partner will develop.
◆ Research suggests that active fathers have better overall health themselves.

Advantages to your children

◆ They will not grow up with set ideas about sex roles.
◆ They will build up good relationships with both parents.

◆ They will not be too dependent on one parent for emotional support.

◆ They will gain from the individual strengths of each parent.

Advantages to you

◆ Shared responsibilities for the home and family will reduce your stress levels.

◆ You will be able to maintain a better balance and control of your time.

◆ Your partner will appreciate what you do.

◆ You will feel secure in the knowledge that your partner is perfectly capable in your absence.

How to put your partner off

Criticising, interfering and nagging (the original CIN)

Always stand back and remind yourself what your overall aim is. Firstly, what your partner is doing should be giving you time and energy for something else. Secondly, there will be a particular aim for whatever task your partner is doing. If you are doing something else and your partner is getting on with the job of parenting or household chores then all should be well. It does not matter *how* his job gets done as long as the end result is acceptable. Acceptable may not mean exactly up to your standard, in which case concentrate on praising what he has done and building up from there.

Hovering

Hovering nearby is not good time management – you might as well do the task yourself. Apart from this, your partner may interpret this as criticism or pending criticism. If you used to take more responsibility for child care or household chores, then you may want to do tackle some tasks together on the first occasion. But not on the second.

Saying 'I do it this way . . .'

Your partner is bound to develop his own way of doing things. He does not have to be a clone of you or a highly trained assistant. So what if the children have their bath before tea, if he hoovers the curtains or if your daughter is dressed in her sister's yellow skirt and 'matching' pink pyjama top.

Interrogation

If your partner has truly taken on a task as his own, not only will you refrain from hovering or interfering at the time but you will have to stop yourself from interrogating your partner afterwards. If your partner has been looking after the children, you will clearly want to know what they have been up to. This is different from endless questions along the lines of 'Did you remember to . . .?' or 'Why haven't you . . .?'

Giving detailed written instructions

There may be a case for leaving your partner with some written reminders about doctor's appointments and the like. But it can be patronising and offputting to leave a list of things to do in the house and a list of dos and don'ts concerning the children.

Taking over

You may arrive home or finish another task earlier than you expected. This does not mean you have to take over from your partner, thus undermining his confidence and making him feel like an assistant, not an equal parent.

Using Daddy as the ultimate threat

The days have hopefully gone when we say 'Just wait until your father gets home' but it can be tempting when things get on top of you. However, your partner does not want to be seen as 'the bad guy' and this will not help you or your children either. Make sure you are consistent with each other when it comes to discipline and that you support each other when necessary.

Using your partner as a servant

You should be equal partners in child care and joint occupiers of your property. Neither of you will want one partner to be making all the decisions while the other merely carries out the orders. Sit down and make major decisions and accept his own decisions concerning the minor everyday problems which may arise while he is doing the parenting. It is easy to fall into the trap of talking to each other like servants – the occasional 'Please' and 'Thank you' would not go amiss.

Handing him the same child every time

When a new baby comes along, it is all too easy to hand the eldest to your partner so you can get along with mothering the baby. Everyone gains from each child spending time with each parent and hopefully everyone spending time all together now and again!

Panicking

It may all go wrong one day, especially if your partner is getting used to a new role. Your jumper may have shrunk in the washing machine, the baby's nappy may have fallen off and your eldest child may have gone to school without her lunch box. Do not panic but try to talk about how to make it go more smoothly the next time. You will be able to laugh about it – eventually.

HOW TO ENCOURAGE YOUR PARTNER

Make decisions together

Decide your roles and the division of labour together. It would be unfair for one parent to have all the 'good' jobs but on the other hand you will both have preferences as well as personal strengths Review the arrangement at agreed intervals so you can ensure that it is working well for everyone.

Be flexible

Although you will want some very specific divisions of labour, you will need to be flexible about these. You or your partner may go through very busy periods at work or even periods of ill health. Think in terms of the home and parenting tasks being shared in a structured way rather than being divided.

Give praise

This will give your partner confidence, particularly if he is taking over some of your original roles. Praise his efforts, make sure he develops good self-esteem as a father and tell him he is needed, in fact essential. Encourage your children to show their appreciation too. Hopefully you will get some praise of your own.

Do not expect perfection

There is no such thing as a perfect parent. Let your partner do his best with enjoyment. He will do things his way and so much the better for your child. You do not want a duplicate of yourself so do not expect one.

Exploit his talents

Your partner may actually do some things better than you. He is bound to have his own strengths so acknowledge these and let him do the things he is best at. However, some fathers show a stronger preference for the parenting and less for the domestic chores. Your circumstances may mean that he will need to be involved in both – so make sure he is.

Consult him

You will, of course, want to make decisions together. This will also help your partner feel a sense of worth, knowing that when it comes to the home and family, he is not just second in command but an equal partner. This will help him take on his share of the responsibility as well as the chores. Even in an equal partnership, it is so often the mother who knows when the children's feet need measuring or when injections are due. A discussion along the lines of 'Do you think Tom's feet have grown?' may lead to a greater share in the decision making.

Give him a break

In fact, give each other a break. Shared parenting may enable you both to work but it should also enable you both to relax as well. See if you can schedule in times when each of you can have time alone. Hopefully, you can also spend some time out together, so have one or two reliable babysitters to hand.

Explain about your work to the children

Explain about your partner's work too. Sometimes, the emphasis is to explain what Mummy does and why she cannot always be there. It helps the children to understand more about Daddy's work too. As they mature, they will gain more understanding about you and your partner's emotions, tiredness and personal needs – but do not expect too much too soon.

SEPARATED PARENTING

If you are divorced or separated, you will still want to make the most of your children's father, whatever your emotional feelings might be. Your children will want to continue having a relationship with both parents and this can work well for you too. Put the past behind you and sit down to discuss your shared responsibilities. Your ex-partner will not want to feel 'used' but, on the other hand, you should be able to work out an arrangement which suits you all. It is probably in your ex-partner's interest that you work as well as yours, so ask him if he is prepared to help out during busy work periods. The other strategies for encouraging partners also work in these circumstances including praise, encouragement and avoiding criticism.

SHARING THE FIVE-MINUTE APPROACH

If you are going to adopt good time-management techniques, then it would help if your partner shares in this. It is hopeless deciding to make lists of priorities only to find that your partner has very different priorities from you. Far better to discuss them together right from the start. Make sure your partner also has realistic expectations of your dual role, that he includes parenting in his list of priorities and that he does not want or expect you to be some sort of super-parent.

YOU KNOW YOU'VE SUCCEEDED WHEN . . .

◆ Your partner starts showing *you* how *he* changes the nappies.
◆ Your child is just as likely to ask for Daddy when he wakes at night.

- Your partner notices when something needs doing and does not wait to be asked.
- Your son imitates Daddy doing the dusting.
- You feel in control of your time.
- You and your partner *both* feel you have established a good balance between all the facets of your life.
- Your partner takes the children to get their feet measured for possible new shoes.
- Time to yourself is not only in your list of priorities, it's in your partner's too.
- Everything runs smoothly most of the time but it does not matter when it doesn't.
- Someone asks if your husband works too.

'DO YOU HAVE A SUPPORTIVE PARTNER?'

Parents answered . . .

'Yes, he does everything for Jegan that I can do – except for breast feeding!'

Kathleen N'Dow

(*Note*: You can express your milk and feed it from a bottle to give your partner a share of the feeding.)

'I would like him to be more intuitive about household chores.'
Gillian Walsh

'Yes, he does whatever he's asked to do. I would like him to volunteer more or think for himself what is required, rather than wait to be asked.'

Lynne Macleod

'I would like him to take a more positive role instead of asking me what has to be done.'

Winnie Taylor

(*Note*: These last three quotes are typical of many answers. It suggests mothers need to be more definite and assertive when it comes to total and long-term delegation.)

'When it comes down to a choice and there is an important meeting, my husband has more important meetings than me.'

Fiona Keating

'It would be nice if he could be home earlier during the week to spend more time with Jamie.'

Carol Dronside

(*Note*: Help your partner to set his own priorities. Sadly, the attitude of his work place may be restrictive.)

'He could help more in the house but does well with the children.'

Gina Browning

(*Note*: Another typical answer and one which may need further discussion with your partner.)

'It's not the physical work but the thinking and organising that is so stressful.'

June Foote

'I don't think he could do what I do.'

Diana Smith

(*Note*: Try going away for the weekend and note the appreciation when you return.)

TIME TIPS

- ◆ As soon as you are pregnant, get your partner to lobby his employers for paternity leave.
- ◆ If your partner is resistant to your returning to work, get him to agree to a three- or four-month trial. However, you will need his support so do not try to do everything yourself just to get him on your side.
- ◆ Remember that the alternative to delegation is to do it yourself or not do it at all.

- If your partner asks what he should give the children for tea, the answer is 'What do you think they might like?', not 'Fish fingers and Jane likes hers cut up, Jack likes two and please give Jenny the Winnie-the-Pooh plate.'
- Discuss the possibility of your partner having his main meal at lunch-time.
- Do not expect the mornings to include detailed discussions with your partner – this is usually the busiest time for everyone.
- Have a rule that you will say a pleasant goodbye to each other, however rushed and stressful the occasion.
- Have a joint desk diary/calender or have a diary meeting once a week so that you each know about extra work commitments or appointments at your child's school or nursery.
- Do some tasks together, for example you could do the ironing in front of a favourite TV programme, taking it in turns to sit behind the ironing board.
- Take it turns to get up first at weekends. Each of you could have a lie-in on one weekend day.
- Schedule in some time you can spend together away from work and children.

FIVE-MINUTE CHECKLIST: DO YOU MAKE THE MOST OF YOUR PARTNER?

- DOES YOUR PARTNER CHECK WITH YOU BEFORE HE STARTS A HOUSEHOLD CHORE?

- DO YOU SOMETIMES FIND YOU HAVE BOTH DONE THE SAME JOB?

- IS IT SOMETIMES EASIER TO DO IT YOURSELF?

- DO YOU EVER TELEPHONE TO CHECK THAT EVERYTHING IS GOING SMOOTHLY IN YOUR ABSENCE?

◆ ARE THERE CERTAIN THINGS WHICH ARE SO MUCH YOUR JOB THAT YOU COULD NEVER DELEGATE THEM?

◆ DO YOU START GIVING YOUR PARTNER A LIST OF DUTIES AS SOON AS HE SETS FOOT IN THE DOOR?

◆ DO YOU WISH YOU HAD YOUR PARTNER'S EASIER LIFESTYLE?

◆ DO YOU THREATEN YOUR PARTNER THAT YOU WILL NOT BE ATTENDING HIS OFFICE FUNCTION, DO YOU HIDE HIS FAVOURITE DRINK OR DO YOU WITHDRAW 'CONJUGAL RIGHTS' IN AN EFFORT TO GET HIS HELP?

◆ DO YOU EXPECT YOUR PARTNER TO GIVE UP HIS FAVOURITE HOBBY?

◆ DOES YOUR PARTNER MOAN ABOUT CERTAIN TASKS?

◆ DO YOU ACKNOWLEDGE THAT YOUR PARTNER CAN DO SOME THINGS BETTER THAN YOU?

◆ ARE YOU ABLE TO RELAX AND PUT YOUR FEET UP EVEN WHEN THE ROOM YOU ARE IN HAS NOT BEEN TIDIED TO YOUR LIKING?

◆ DOES YOUR PARTNER SOMETIMES CLEAN THE TOILET?

◆ ARE YOU ABLE TO PUT YOUR FEET UP, EVEN WHEN YOUR PARTNER IS STILL BUSY?

◆ DO YOU AND YOUR PARTNER HAVE TIME FOR EACH OTHER?

◆ DO YOU PARTICIPATE IN ACTIVITIES WHICH MAY TRADITIONALLY HAVE BEEN DONE BY A MAN – SUCH AS CHECKING THE CAR?

◆ DO YOU DIVIDE UP THE TASKS ACCORDING TO YOUR INDIVIDUAL NEEDS AND CIRCUMSTANCES RATHER THAN ACCORDING TO SOCIETY'S TRADITIONS?

◆ DO YOUR LONG-TERM PRIORITIES MORE OR LESS MATCH YOUR PARTNER'S?

◆ CAN YOUR PARTNER CHANGE HIS ARRANGEMENTS AT THE LAST MINUTE?

◆ DOES YOUR PARTNER KNOW THE NAME OF YOUR CHILD'S TEACHER/ CHILD MINDER/DOCTOR/DENTIST/HEALTH VISITOR/BEST FRIENDS?

Answering 'no' to the first 10 questions and 'yes' to the rest suggests an ideal partnership. Do not worry if yours is not quite ideal – very few are.

CHAPTER TEN

How Not to be a 24-Hour Mum

'She generally gave herself very good advice (though she seldom followed it).'

Lewis Carroll

If you are a parent, then you are a parent 24 hours a day. However, this does not mean you are on duty 24 hours a day with no time for anything else at all. And even if, at times, you are on a 24-hour shift, parenting can be part of the rest of your life. A five-minute mum does not claim to be a mum in five minutes, she just claims to be in control of every five minutes of the day. A 24-hour mum, on the other hand is totally out of control. She feels that she ought to be on duty 24 hours a day or else her child might suffer in some way. She sees herself as indispensable and is herself dependent on her child. She expects nothing short of perfection from herself and cannot trust anyone else to 'do it like she does'. She also uses her time so poorly that she does, indeed, need 24 hours a day to get everything done. With no time-management skills, the parenting and chores just expand to fill the time available.

STRESS

A 24-hour hour mum has unrealistic aims, making life very stressful indeed. A 24-hour mum feels out of control, that nothing will get done and that life is a muddle. This, too, can be very stressful. Stress means tension, tiredness, irritability and even illness. Busy parents may put these feelings of stress down to just having too much to do. But being busy does not have to cause stress. By being a five-minute mum, and therefore in control of the hours in the day, stress can be reduced even for the busiest parent.

Different people respond differently to stress and for most people, not all stress is bad. It can prevent lethargy and stop you from procrastinating. In other words, a little stress can get a lot done. But a lot of stress can stop any achievement altogether.

Stress squashers

♦ Keep fit. Exercise prevents stress.
♦ Talk to your friends, family or anyone in a similar situation or lifestyle to your own.
♦ Set aside some time each day to do some specific relaxation. If you have ever attended prenatal classes, you should already know one relaxation technique. Otherwise there are endless courses or books to help.
♦ Develop an 'instant relaxation' technique. This might involve taking a deep breath and letting it out slowly as all your muscles 'drop down' or relax. Use this whenever you are faced with a sudden stressful situation.
♦ Take a break each day.
♦ Make sure that you get enough sleep. If tension and stress are preventing you from getting to sleep, try doing your relaxation exercises last thing at night.
♦ Take time over meals.
♦ Try the time-management techniques outlined in Chapter 7.
♦ Accept what cannot be changed and change what needs to be changed.

REALISTIC AIMS

The life of a five-minute mum should be flexible and unstressful. Five-minute solutions should make life easier for all the family.

24-hour solution: Have daily organised activities starting promptly at 9.00 a.m.

5-minute solution: Allow your children time with others and on their own. Know when your child will respond best to a special time with you each day.

24-hour solution: Deal with behaviour problems with a chart of rules to be strictly adhered to at all times.
5-minute solution: Have a consistent policy for dealing with behaviour, with allowances made for tiredness and special circumstances.

24-hour solution: Have a wall chart of child development with daily goals for your child's achievements.
5-minute solution: Be aware of your child's stage of development and have some appropriate games handy at all times for when you both feel like playing.

24-hour solution: Ensure your child joins every available club and organisation.
5-minute solution: Be realistic about what your child can join. Allow her to follow up any particular interests but have some time without organised activity.

24-hour solution: Ensure your life revolves around the needs of the children.
5-minute solution: Allow the needs of the children to have a high priority but schedule time for yourself and your partner too.

24-hour solution: Make yourself available to your child at all times.
5-minute solution: Make yourself available when you realistically can but know the benefits your child gains from sometimes being in the care of others.

HUMOUR

Humour is such a successful stress squasher that it deserves to be taken seriously. Medical and psychological research prove that smiling and laughing really are the best medicine. A laugh a day keeps the doctor away – and it's free, available to everyone and has only beneficial long-term side-effects. There will be times for a busy parent where you have either to laugh or cry. Crying is not bad – sometimes 'letting it all out' can also reduce stress. But whenever you can, choose laughter.

'WHAT MAKES YOU LAUGH?'

Parents answered . . .

'Getting Mother's Day and Easter cards from my four-month-old since he has started at his nursery.'

Kathleen N'Dow

'Rory calling me Amanda (nursery nurse) and calling Amanda mummy.'

Lynne Macleod

'Both girls complaining on the days I don't work because Lorraine (the nanny) isn't there!'

Anne Anderson

'Arriving to take my daughter home from the child minder's to find that she did not want to go home in the car. She had just been in a bus, complete with a driver in a cap. How could I compete?'

Winnie Taylor

'Victoria calling her day nursery the office.'

Tom Stubbs

'My neighbour referring to my daughter as 'poor Claire' because she has to go to a fantastic nursery three days a week and has a mum who can afford to take her on nice holidays!'

Sarah Hall

'Jacob explaining to his friends that he has two working mothers. Well, I suppose he does!'

Geoff Standish

Note that even in the examples here, there are at least three 'laugh or cry' situations. So, like these parents, try laughing when your neighbour makes her views known, when your child calls you by her carer's name or when something about their day care is actually so good, they miss it or want you to provide it too.

FIVE-MINUTE CHECKLIST: ARE YOU A CLOSET 24-HOUR MUM?

◆ HAVE YOU KEPT UP WITH ALL YOUR OLD FRIENDS REGARDLESS OF WHETHER THEY HAVE CHILDREN OR NOT?

◆ DO YOU CONSTANTLY WORRY ABOUT YOUR CHILD WHEN HE IS IN THE CARE OF OTHERS BECAUSE HE CAN ONLY REALLY RELATE TO YOU?

◆ DO YOU WISH YOU DID NOT HAVE TO WORK OR ARE YOU RELUCTANT TO RETURN TO WORK EVEN THOUGH YOU HAVE A CAREER YOU PREVIOUSLY ENJOYED?

◆ DO YOU HAVE AT LEAST ONE HOBBY OR INTEREST WHICH DOES NOT INVOLVE THE REST OF THE FAMILY?

◆ WOULD YOU LIKE TO RETURN TO WORK/TAKE UP AN INTEREST/WORK LONGER HOURS BUT YOU JUST DO NOT HAVE THE TIME?

◆ DO YOU LOOK FORWARD TO WHEN YOU HAVE TIME FOR YOURSELF?

◆ DO YOU CONSTANTLY FIND YOURSELF SAYING 'WHEN THE CHILDREN ARE OLDER . . .'?

◆ ARE YOU ALREADY DREADING THE TIME WHEN YOUR CHILD WILL SPEND MORE HOURS OUT WITH HIS FRIENDS THAN AT HOME WITH YOU?

◆ ARE YOU CONSTANTLY BUSY AND YET NEVER HAVE ENOUGH TIME?

◆ ARE THERE ENOUGH HOURS IN THE DAY OR COULD YOU DO WITH ONE OR TWO EXTRA?

Useful Addresses

Acre (Action with
   Communitites in Rural
   England)
Stroud Road
Cirencester
GLOS
GL7 6JR
Tel: 0285 653477

British Activity Holiday
   Association
22 Green Lane
Hersham
Walton on Thames
SURREY
KT12 5HD
Tel: 0932 252994

British Association for Early
   Education (Baece)
111 City View House
463 Bethnal Green Road
LONDON
E2 9QH
Tel: 071-739 7594

Career Development Loans
Freepost
NEWCASTLE UPON
   TYNE X
NE85 1BR

Childcare Association
8 Talbot Road
LONDON
N6 4QR
Tel: 081-348 2800

Childcare Cheques
Mercer Fraser
Metropolitan House
   Northgate
Chichester
WEST SUSSEX
PO19 1BE
Tel: 0243 532000

Childcare Vouchers
   Ltd/Childcare Solutions
50 Vauxhall Bridge Road
LONDON
SW1V 2RS
Tel: 071-834 6666

Choices in Childcare
14–18 West Bar Green
Sheffield
YORKSHIRE
S1 2DA
Tel: 0742 766881

Daycare Trust
Wesley House
4 Wild Court
LONDON
WC2B 5AU
Tel: 071-405 5617

**Department of Health
Publications Unit**
No. 2 Site
Heywood Stores
Manchester Road
Heywood
LANCASHIRE
OL10 2D2

DSS Leaflets
P.O. Box 21
Stanmore
MIDDLESEX
HA7 1AY

**Educational Guidance For
Adults**
P.O. Box 109
Hatfield Polytechnic
HERTS
Tel: 07072 79499

**Equal Opportunites
Commission**
Overseas House
Quay Street
MANCHESTER
M3 33HN
Tel: 061-833 9244

**Federation of Recruitment
and Employment Services**
36 Mortimer Street
LONDON
W1N 7RB

Further Education Unit
Department of Education and
Science
Elizabeth House
York Road
LONDON
SE1 7PH
Tel: 071-934 9412

**Home Office, Immigration
and Nationality
Department**
Lunar House
40 Wellesley Road
Croydon
SURREY
CRO 4BY
Tel: 081-686 0688

**Kids Clubs Network/
National Out of School
Alliance**
271–281 Whitechapel Road
LONDON
E1 1BY
Tel: 071-247 3009

La Leche League
BM3424
LONDON
WC1N 3XX
Tel: 071-242 1278

Maternity Alliance
15 Britannia Stret
LONDON
WC1X 9JN
Tel: 071-837 1265

National Childbirth Trust
Alexandra House
Oldham Terrace
Acton
LONDON
W3 6NH
Tel: 081-992 8637

National Childcare
  Campaign/Childcare Now
Wesley House
4 Wild Court
LONDON
WC2B 5AU
Tel: 071-405 5617

National Childcare Directory
1 Ickleton Road
Wantage
OXFORD
OX12 9JA
Tel: 0235 768827

National Childminding
  Association
8 Masons Hill
Bromley
KENT
BR2 9EY
Tel: 081-464 6164

National Institute of Adult
  Continuing Education
19b De Montfort Street
LEICESTER
LE1 7GE
Tel: 0533 551451

National Playing Fields
  Association
25 Ovington Square
LONDON
SW3 1LQ
Tel: 071-584 6445

New Ways to Work
309 Upper Street
LONDON
N1 2TY
Tel: 071-226 4026

Parent Network/Parent-Link
44–46 Caversham Road
LONDON
NW5 2DS
Tel: 071-485 8535

Parents at Work
77 Holloway Road
LONDON
N7 8JZ
Tel: 071-700 5771/2

Pre-School Playgroups
  Association
61–63 Kings Cross Road
LONDON
WC1X 9LL
Tel: 071-833 0991

Universal Aunts Ltd
P.O. Box 304
LONDON
SW4 0NN
Tel: 071-738 8937

Voluntary Organisations
  Liaison Council for Under
  Fives (Volcuf)
77 Holloway Road
LONDON
N7 8JZ
Tel: 071-607 9573

Women's Enterprise
  Development Agency
Aston Science Park
Love Lane
Aston Triangle
BIRMINGHAM
B7 4B5

Working For Childcare
77 Holloway Road
LONDON
N7 8JZ
Tel: 071-700 0281

Women Returners Network
8 John Adam Street
LONDON
WC2N 6EZ
Tel: 071-839 8188

And Finally ...

It is easy to read a book like this and end up with good intentions to put some of the time management ideas into practice. It is quite another thing to actually carry those intentions out. The first step is to acknowledge that there are areas in your life which need changing and that there are parts of your routine which could be approached more effectively. The next step is to start making changes – but gradually.

We all make new year's resolutions every January but how many of us actually stick to them for more than a few days? The easiest resolutions to keep are often the most specific – 'I will not eat any more biscuits at coffee break' or 'I will cut down to five cigarettes a day'. More vague resolutions such as 'I will try to lose weight' or 'I will cut down on smoking' are more likely to be broken. Similarly, if we try to make many good intentions at once, our success rate is likely to be very poor – we always do better if we can concentrate on only the one.

Time management should be tackled in the same way as making good new year's resolutions. Make your aims very specific and take one step at a time. You should also have the overall aim at the back of your mind. The resolution of cutting down to five cigarettes is only a step towards cutting out smoking altogether. So when you feel bogged down in work and parenting, remember why you chose to be a parent and why you do the other things in your life too. Yes, there will always be times when we find it hard to remember why we had children so keep a happy book to hand for those moments. Stick in your favourite snaps of the children and keep a note of all those special, magical moments. Your happy book should be kept where you can get it out quickly in an emergency. For being a parent is one of the most rewarding and enjoyable parts of anyone's life. However, it can be even better when we have the time to really enjoy it. That time is available, so start Mum's great juggling act now, and good luck ...

Index